Is Biden Really Too Old?
The Politics of Age and Ageism in America

Earl Ofari Hutchinson

Middle Passage Press
Los Angeles, CA

Publisher's Cataloging-in-Publication Data

Names: Hutchinson, Earl Ofari.

Title: Is Biden really too old? The politics of age and ageism in America / Earl Ofari Hutchinson.

Description: Los Angeles, CA : Middle Passage Press, 2024. | Includes bibliographic references and index.

Identifiers: LCCN 2023923429 | ISBN 9798892691833 (pbk.)

Subjects: LCSH: Biden, Joseph R. | Trump, Donald, 1946- . | Ageism – United States. | Presidents – Term of office – United States. | Political leadership – Age factors. | Older politicians. | BISAC: POLITICAL SCIENCE / American Government / Executive Branch. | POLITICAL SCIENCE / Political Process / Campaigns & Elections. | POLITICAL SCIENCE / Political Process / Media & Internet.

Classification: LCC JK550 H88 2024 | DDC 323.5 H--dc23

LC record available at https://lccn.loc.gov/2023923429

Table of Contents

Introduction

In the second presidential debate on October 21, 1984, between incumbent President Ronald Reagan and his Democratic opponent Walter Mondale, Reagan was asked by the moderator, Henry Trewhitt of the Baltimore Sun, about his advancing age. By then Reagan had repeatedly been continually reminded by much of the media and political observers that he was the "oldest president in history" at age seventy-three.

Trewhitt's question: "Is there any doubt in your mind that you would be able to function in such circumstances?" Reagan's memorable answer:

"I will not make age an issue of this campaign. I am not going to exploit, for political purposes, my opponent's youth and inexperience."

Whatever slender chance Mondale had to upend the popular incumbent Reagan went down the drain with that devastating retort. However, in the decades since Reagan's sharp quip on age, it hasn't stopped innumerable political pundits, many in the media, and a large segment of the public from obsessing over age and claiming or worrying that age is a problem in a politician.

In June 2022, the contrarian *Washington Free Beacon*, for instance, compiled a list of quotes from a litany of political pundits, Democratic officials, and Democratic political insiders. The group was asked just one question at various times and by various interviewers, "Is Biden too old to run for a second term?"

The respondents were virtually unanimous on two points. First, they questioned whether he was too old. Second, they questioned whether he could do the presidential job in a second go-round.

More than one year later on November 20, 2023, Biden turned eighty-one. But the concern of many about his age and running again had not changed. The twist this time was the poll on Biden running again did not sample opinion from the general public but from Democrats. Forty percent of them in a *Messenger/Harris* poll said he should not seek a second term. The silver lining in the age cloud was that the dissenters had no one else other than Biden to turn to.

*****

Biden was not one who had any reservations that his age would impede a return run. He'd approach age eighty-two if reelected in November 2024. But Biden reached back into time and took a page from Reagan's famous quip when confronted with the age issue. He pointed to his experience as Reagan did.

His press secretary Karine Jean-Pierre was blunt: "What we say is we have to judge him by what he's done, not by his numbers. I would put the president's stamina, the president's wisdom, and ability to get this done on behalf of the American people, against anyone. Anyone, any day of the week."

Biden simply made a joke about it, "By the way, it's my birthday today. I just want you to know, it's difficult turning sixty." Biden would need all the humor he could muster. He would need to keep citing his experience as a comeback to defuse what repeated polls found—his age continued to be the number one concern among a majority of voters.

His likely 2024 GOP opponent, former President Donald Trump, was also "long in the tooth" at age seventy-seven. Yet, nowhere near the number of voters who thought Biden was too old said the same about Trump.

Trump was not unmindful of the age issue. He took the occasion of Biden's birthday to release a letter from his physician which called Trump's health "excellent."

*****

In *Is Biden Really Too Old? The Politics of Age and Ageism in America*, political analyst Earl Ofari Hutchinson takes a laser sharp look at the great debate over Biden's age. He assesses how much of a liability age poses for Biden. He examines how Reagan and 2008 GOP presidential candidate John McCain dealt with the age issue. He presents the varying views of medical professionals about Biden's age as a factor. He details research and studies on aging and the performance of older Americans.

He examines the negative stereotypes, views, and typecasting of older Americans depicted in advertising, films, and much of the media, and voiced by many Americans. He details what the Constitution and the Founding Fathers wrote and said about age and politics. Hutchinson contends that aging has had a profound effect on American politics. Finally, he asks whether age would be the deal breaker for Biden in his bid to stay in the Oval Office in 2024.

1

How Old is Too Old?

In April 2023, Biden announced that he would run for a second term in the Oval Office. Practically in the next breath, he tried to take the inevitable age question off the table. He was blunt, saying "age doesn't register with me."

"They're going to see a race, and they're going to judge whether or not I have it or don't have it." He meant of course the voters. He continued, "I respect them taking a hard look at it. I'd take a hard look at it as well. I took a hard look at it before I decided to run."

Biden well knew it would take more than his perfunctory dismissal of age as an issue in the campaign to make it go away. In November 2023, it was plopped back on the table by a seemingly unlikely source. That was former President Obama's key advisor, David Axelrod, a Democratic Party stalwart. He caused a minor stir when he told an interviewer, "I think he has a 50-50 shot here, but no better than that, maybe a little worse. He thinks he can cheat nature here and it's really risky." Axelrod's slap at Biden on the age issue drew a mix of criticism and agreement from Democrats.

Biden did not comment. However, there was little doubt that he was not unmindful of Axelrod and the repeated knocks from other Democrats about his age. Yet, it was something that others worried about; he wasn't one of them. Close friends all agreed that he felt that if he was fit and healthy, he would continue to be politically active.

Biden though took no chances. In February 2023, he voluntarily released a medical report from November 2021, almost one year into his term, that judged him as "healthy" and "vigorous" and said he was "fit to successfully execute the duties of the Presidency." The report was updated in February 2023. It found no change in his health and fitness.

*****

Biden had more than just his positive medical report to back up his contention that an eighty-year-old plus president was not at best a risk and at worst a clear and present danger. There was a virtual growth industry within the medical/science industry that continually debunked many of the long-held myths about aging. One was the number of the aged. The numbers were getting larger and larger each year.

In a 2020 survey on global aging, the World Health Organization (WHO) estimated that "Between 2000 and 2050, the proportion of the world's population over sixty years would double from about eleven to twenty percent."

Additional studies showed that there was no inherent inevitability of total mental and physical collapse due to age. It was also possible to reverse some of the most dreaded conditions routinely associated with aging. Maintaining an active lifestyle, healthy diet, and mental and social engagement are vital to sustaining good health, which is true at any age. Some studies showed it was also possible to peel back some of the aging process. Studies cited the increasingly popular use of cognitive training techniques and regular resistance-type exercises that could sharpen cognitive abilities, slow loss of muscle mass, and maintain bone density.

The number of individuals aged sixty-plus in America was growing for a reason. More individuals were boosting their health by adopting a healthy diet, increasing regular exercise, and staying engaged in various activities. An added factor was how individuals perceived the aging process.

Studies showed that individuals who viewed aging as a positive, rather than as something to fear and dread, were far more likely to recover faster from a severe disability that might result from falls or other physical mishaps than an individual who was afraid of aging. If an individual regarded aging as a natural part of life, without fear and worry, this measurably increased their physical and, most especially, their mental wellness. This is not solely a matter of mind over matter. Scientists concluded that a regular physical exercise regimen increased "dynamic muscle strength, muscle size, and functional capacity." It also reduced the risk of Alzheimer's disease and other forms of dementia.

*****

This latter point that age in and of itself did not automatically put older persons in danger of developing Alzheimer's or dementia was crucial to note. The negative drumbeat focusing on Biden's age was that he was virtually on the verge of dementia.

Typical was the reaction to Biden's speech at a campaign reception in Manhattan in September 2023, when a reporter cherry-picked this snippet from his talk, "So, I decided I would run. And it became—I ran because I thought everything this country stood for was up for grabs for the first time in my career." The fact that Biden repeated that he would run in the same sentence was supposedly conclusive proof as a clear sign of dementia or Alzheimer's.

The writer cited mental health experts who said that repeating words, phrases, or stories in a short time frame could be a potential sign of cognitive decline. To underscore the supposed evidence of Biden's slipping into dementia the writer cited a handful of tweets from Twitter users:

"The gerbil on the wheel in his head died a long time ago. The wheel is rusting and collecting cobwebs." Another user commented, "It's truly concerning how often he repeats himself word-for-word. I mean, is he even fit for office?" And yet another wrote, "That's the first sign that I knew an aunt had Alzheimer's. We had the same conversation every twenty minutes."

It seemed ridiculous on the surface to dredge up Twitter users as the ultimate authorities on mental health issues. However, when the buzzwords "dementia" and "Alzheimer's" were attached to Biden by more than a few in the media and many top politicos, it made frightening sense to many.

The one obvious counter to the charge of Biden slipping into incoherence was seldom mentioned by many political analysts: that was Biden's impressive legislative track record. One commentator did walk through the checklist of those achievements, saying "He passed a bipartisan $1 trillion infrastructure bill $1 trillion in November 2021—a package that many Republicans are now touting as a success, even though they voted against it. He passed bipartisan gun control legislation in 2022, to the fury of the Republican base. And he negotiated a debt ceiling increase with minimal concessions, again infuriating Republican hard-liners."

He drew the obvious conclusion from Biden's legislative success story, namely that someone who had badly lost their way mentally would not have had even the remotest chance of pulling off those successes. Biden's cognitive skills must still be intact, no matter how often he garbled a word or sentence.

The popular belief fed by much of the media was that dementia was an inevitable part of getting old. This was continually disproven by medical experts and in studies. The WHO study found that most older adults both within and without the U.S. did not have and would not develop dementia. The study further found that even if an individual showed signs of cognitive decline, that did not mean it would develop into full-blown dementia. The key factors remained diet, exercise, and continued engagement with others. This does much to slow down any cognitive impairment.

*****

Biden had a far bigger problem with the obsession the media, many Democrats, and much of the public had with his age. The issue was the widespread, and deeply ingrained belief that aging was a negative thing, something to approach and regard with terror.

By the start of Biden's first term, there was a storehouse of studies that confirmed that older persons were fitter, more active, and had lost little of their capacity to still function at a high level. Gerontologists even branded this the "longevity dividend." It didn't matter. It did not shake the perception of many that an older person had lost zest and a positive outlook on life.

Thus Marc Sigel, a medical director and conservative medical issues commentator, suggested that Biden should have been required to take a cognitive test, based on that mistaken popular belief about aging. His added source for making that demand was, of all people, Trump: "I agree with what President Trump told me during an interview at the White House in July 2020—that those elderly individuals who would be president should take a cognitive test (as he said he had) as part of a routine physical."

There was little doubt that Sigel wouldn't be alone in shouting for Biden to submit to such an exam during the 2024 campaign. He and others had already asked and answered the question "How old is too old?"

Their answer was that Biden was just that: "too old." The real question, though, was whether that answer was based on objective medical science or was it partisan politics talking?

2

The War on the Aged

In June 2020, six months before Biden took office, a study by the *Framework Institute*, "Gauging Aging: Mapping the Gaps between Expert and Public Understandings of Aging in America," confirmed the deep-seated public bias about the effects of aging. The study found that even when individuals worked diligently to maintain a healthy lifestyle, many still believed that their health would inevitably fall apart sooner rather than later.

This was an example of the proverbial self-fulfilling prophecy. If you believed something to be a fact, despite all evidence to the contrary, perception always won out over reality. It was no different with the aging issue. The media ran nonstop ads that played up youth, constantly equating it with health and vigor, while openly and subtly disparaging the aged.

Here is just a tiny sliver of such commonplace ads:

- A Get Out the Vote ad urged young people to get out to vote. Older persons are depicted as selfish, uncaring, and out-of-touch people who are doing everything to ruin the future as they lack even an ounce of concern for the young.

- An E-Trade ad depicted older people as buffoonish and incompetent in a range of jobs. The message was that they are way out of their depth in many jobs, which are best left to younger people.

- A Medicare ad showed an older woman who is cranky and irritable. She is reviled by friends and foes alike.

- A Duracell ad showed an older man seemingly mindlessly wandering around a beach with a metal detector. Toward the end of the commercial, the man can hardly stand up. The effort of walking around for a short period simply proved to be too taxing and he needs a battery that can give him more added-on years.

- A Volkswagen ad depicted an older woman offering her car for sale. In flashbacks, it showed her careening about seemingly recklessly in the car. The message is to look out for older people when they drive—one might be taking their life in their hands.

- A Tide ad showed a doddering grandfatherly type coming into his relative's house dressed in nothing but his underwear. The message was that older people are typically disoriented.

That wasn't all. Many commercial advertisers also made older persons the butt of put-downs, jokes, and ridicule. "Some may think it's cute and harmless to make fun of older adults, to make light of their age and experience," noted Paul Irvin, chairman of the Milken Institute Center for the Future of Aging. "I think that if you did that same ad with stereotyped images of women, people of color, or LGBTQ individuals, there would be outrage, and rightly so."

*****

This deliberate bias against older persons in commercial depictions continued to fuel the stereotypes about aging. This also had an inevitable effect on older adults. Many of them believed the stereotypes about themselves. It fostered pessimism and negativity, and ensured that many would throw up their hands and say that eating healthier, exercising more, and thinking positively about life meant little since aging had consigned them to unavoidable disability and death.

These depictions also reinforced discrimination. "Unchallenged stereotypes about aging often fuel ageism," observed the behavioral scientist Rosie Evans-Krimme. "These stereotypes are often depicted as individuals being slower, less tech-savvy, and less resilient, which leads to discrimination in hiring, promotion, and training opportunities. Older workers may be overlooked for leadership positions, assumed to be less innovative, or even passed over for training programs based on their age."

Government agencies and private employers did little to dispel this pessimism. Despite the phalanx of laws that barred age discrimination, it was still a huge barrier to older persons who wanted and were fully capable of finding productive employment. Here's what some older job applicants who weren't hired because of their age told an interviewer:

I'm a 56-year-old IT specialist with a solid track record and résumé, and I've been unemployed for over a year. I estimate I've applied to more than 300 jobs. I'm not sure why I'm not getting them, but I suspect ageism has something to do with it.

In October, I was laid off from a major computer company, where I'd worked for five years, as part of a corporate realignment. Before that, I'd worked at another big tech company for 20 years. I apply for every job for which I'm remotely qualified. And I've had exactly 31 interviews, most with frontline recruiters. I've been a finalist for a job a few times, but it's always gone to someone else, often decades younger.

I've lowered my expectations, and I'm still not having any luck. One company offered me a help-desk position for half the salary I was making. A recruiting coach suggested removing all dates from my résumé and hinted that I start dying my hair.

Employers have a few standard ploys to skirt the law on age discrimination. They may require an applicant to provide their birth date or to provide their graduation date. Many companies require the ability to lift a certain weight or produce a current driver's license. Or, they simply never bother to respond to an older person's job application.

*****

The burden of proof for trying to prove age discrimination in hiring is laid almost exclusively on the older job applicants themselves. The SCOTUS saw to that. In the 2009 case *Gross v. FBL Financial Services Inc.*, the U.S. Supreme Court said plaintiffs suing for violations of the federal Age Discrimination in Employment Act (ADEA) must prove that their age was the primary motivating factor in an employment decision.

An older person who believed age was the reason they were not hired had to navigate an almost impossible phalanx of hurdles to prove that age was the reason for their not being hired. They had to first file a claim with the Equal Employment Opportunity Commission (EEOC) citing the Age Discrimination and Employment Act that prohibited age discrimination in employment. The claim had to be filed within one hundred and eighty to three hundred days of the refusal to hire.

The claimant was required to carefully and meticulously keep and produce records of conversations, interviews, records of any interaction with other employees at the company, and the name and the age of the person who was hired in the place of the claimant.

Then the employer had their say. In telling why the company didn't hire the older applicant, it had an endless storehouse of rationales to throw up in their defense, all of which on the surface seemed to have nothing to do with not hiring the older applicant.

After the age discrimination complaint is filed the wait begins. It often takes months for the EEOC to render a decision. In most cases, the claimant loses. Of the thousands of cases of age discrimination filed annually, less than twenty percent of the claimants won in 2020.

The greatest hurdle was proving intent. The claimant had to prove that the employer deliberately denied employment because the applicant was deemed too old. This was a mountainous barrier to successfully scale. "The difficulty lies in not knowing who got selected, what differentiated that person from you, and whether or not you were more qualified for the role," noted Ray Peeler, an associate legal counsel at the EEOC

In December 2023, a bipartisan group of House members proposed a bill to make it easier for older job applicants to file and win age discrimination lawsuits. There was no indication of any great rush by lawmakers to secure passage.

The one positive that came out of the obsessive attention on Biden's age was that it further spurred medical scientists to examine, debunk, and continue publicly debunking the wrong-headed mythology about aging even more intensely. Biden would remain on the hot seat about his age through the entirety of the 2024 presidential campaign.

As the grim statistics on rampant age discrimination in the workplace showed, he was hardly the only older job applicant who had to fend off talk that he was too old for the job. The only difference between Biden and the countless others who faced discrimination was that the job that many questioned his ability to handle because of age was the nation's top job.

3

The Democrats' Jitters Over Biden's Age

In September 2023, yet another top Democrat stepped into the debate over Biden's age. This time it was the Democrat closest to Biden—his Vice President Kamala Harris. She was asked by an interviewer the then stock question about Biden's age and fitness.

Harris gave what could be construed as a mixed message: "Joe Biden is going to be just fine." However, she didn't stop there. When asked if she was prepared to take over the presidency, she assured, "Yes, I am, if necessary." The question and her answer were another sign that the age issue was something that was on the mind of more than one person in the White House.

Harris, of course, was in the immediate line of presidential succession if Biden faltered. However, the problem she and many other Democrats had was that if Biden was not the candidate again, who could step in as a replacement and ensure that the White House would not tumble back to Trump or another GOP presidential nominee in 2024? Biden made no effort to hide that sentiment.

In a series of fund-raising appearances in December 2023, Biden was candid: "If Trump wasn't running, I'm not sure I'd be running. Democrats cannot let him win." Though he later appeared to slightly walk back the blunt rationale for why he was running again, nonetheless, it was clear that Trump was the prime motivator for his reelection bid. Neither talk of his age nor talk of a replacement had any place in Biden's thinking in that respect.

Many, if not a majority, of top Democrats thought that Harris could not cut the muster as the Democratic contender if Biden stepped aside. The mere thought of her as the nominee struck horror into many of them.

Minnesota congressman, Dean Phillips was one Democrat who was the loudest in demanding that Biden step down because of age. Phillips briefly challenged Biden for the party nomination. He also publicly ripped on Harris, saying "Americans have made the decision that she was not prepared to 'step into' Mr. Biden's shoes. That is not my opinion."

He claimed that he had heard "from others who know her a lot better than I do that many think she's not well positioned." Phillips in turn was ripped by a slew of other Democrats for sowing division within the party.

But Harris, or for that matter Biden's ability to function, was only an issue because of the age question.

*****

Biden, of course, heard the loud grumbling and rumblings of discontent about Harris and pushed back. In September 2023, he quietly asked key Democratic party leaders who had raised doubts about Harris remaining on the ticket why they felt she was a liability. Former House Speaker Nancy Pelosi was one. She quickly made it clear that she had complete confidence in Harris as Biden's VP in 2024, saying "She's very politically astute, I don't think people give her enough credit."

The Harris question notwithstanding, the message from Democratic party leaders in late 2023, then with slightly more than a year to go before the November 2024 election, was "Don't panic." They banked on Biden's positive legislative record of accomplishments and his ability to appeal to the crucial swing state voters as solid pluses. Their political bravado about Biden was for public consumption. The age issue still lurked close to the surface as a major Democratic concern.

In a November 2023 interview, top Obama political strategist David Axelrod drew some heat for intimating that Biden should drop out. He didn't cite age directly as the rationale. But then again, he didn't have to. It was understood that this was the prime concern. Axelrod quickly scrambled and claimed he didn't tell Biden to drop out. "Only @JoeBiden can make this decision," Axelrod wrote on X, the platform previously known as Twitter. "If he continues to run, he will be the nominee of the Democratic Party. What he needs to decide is whether that is wise; whether it's in HIS best interest or the country's?"

Nonetheless, Axelrod's "yes, I did, no I didn't say it" about Biden's re-election chances was in keeping with the underlying unstated worry by many Democrats about Biden's 2024 presidential run. There was no mystery as to why: Democratic party leaders continually read the multiple polls that constantly asked voters about Biden's age. A CNN poll in September 2023 was typical of the findings of most polls taken about Biden's age. A top-heavy percentage of voters flatly said that "Biden is too old to run for president." In a *Reuters/Ipsos* poll in November 2022, nearly half of Democrats thought Biden might not be up to the rigor of another presidential campaign.

Though Trump was just three years younger than Biden, the majority of those polled raised no concern about his age as an election factor. This was doubly odd because many experts who intensely followed and watched Trump did say that age in his case could be a major liability for Trump—not because he was aging, but because of how he acted in his advancing years.

One inveterate Trump watcher pulled no punches in saying that age in Trump's case had worked decidedly against him:

> During Trump's presidency, some of those around him worried that he had lost his mind. Over the years he seemed to grow less and less coherent, more paranoid, more conspiratorial. His speech is erratic, his thoughts disorganized, and he makes simple factual errors—for example, seeming to forget where his father was born. As Trump's years in the Oval Office ticked by, the question of whether there was something neurologically wrong with him became all the more urgent.

> The man says he can't remember even saying he has one of the world's best memories.

Nevertheless, the focus when it came to age as a potential liability remained almost solely on Biden: "Look, Joe Biden should not be their nominee. Joe Biden is unpopular. Joe Biden is too old." Henry Olsen, a senior fellow at the Ethics and Public Policy Center think tank in Washington, summed up the argument regarding "if not Biden, then who else for the Democrats" by saying, "That's no longer a Republican talking point; that's the sentiment of half of the Democratic party and a supermajority of independents, and rational Democrats know that. But the problem is, how do you get rid of the guy?"

*****

That was a problem for another reason: both the obsession with age and its converse—the making a fetish of youth. That was deeply embedded in American culture. Nowhere was this more evident than in the world of advertising. A survey by AARP found that those who created the splashy, chic, youth-oriented ads that almost exclusively target youth consumers were themselves young. The median age for a manager in America's advertising agencies in 2019 was thirty-seven. Those who created the ads were even younger. Their average age was twenty-eight.

The survey further found that even though those over age sixty did the bulk of the spending, they represented only fifteen percent of adults in online media images. And they were seven times more likely than younger adults to be portrayed negatively.

Nothing had changed in 2023 in the run-up to the 2024 presidential election. "There's an enormous opportunity that marketers still don't understand," noted Mike Hodin, former head of global public affairs for Pfizer and now CEO of the Global Coalition on Aging. "Many advertisements treat older adults as dependent and in need of help, rather than as a target market representing substantial revenue growth."

The problem of aging and the deep-seated ageist stereotypes that were glaringly reflected in advertising were hardly exclusively an American phenomenon. In 2005, there was much feverish talk in Europe about a proposal to clamp down on the negative depictions of older people, not to mention the outright ignoring of the aged.

The complaint was the same as in America. The majority of those who created ads were under age thirty and nearly all the advertising either ignored or denigrated older people. However, while the anti-discrimination proposal called public attention to the top-heavy ageist discrimination it bucked up against two equally ingrained problems.

Advertisers want a long-term return on the money they spend on advertising. Their prime concern then was to get a twenty-something person who was likely to buy a particular brand product for years if not decades in the fold. This was a long-term return on their advertising dollars. The same supposedly couldn't be said for targeting a sixty-something-year-old person.

It was also a truism that youth created trends that many others followed and imitated, which included older people. While older people did the bulk of the spending on products, they were influenced by the trends, tastes, and products that younger consumers bought.

It was a noble effort to change perceptions and how advertisers did business. Yet, there was scant evidence that it moved advertisers to suddenly have an epiphany and shift gears on advertising away from the young, let alone any radical shift in how they viewed older persons—namely, still negatively.

That entrenched belief continued to spill over into how Biden was in effect advertised. That was as someone mentally and physically shaky, if not practically senile. That image of him neatly conformed to the still all too prevalent ad world's negative image of the aged.

4

Fun and Games with Biden's Gaffes, Fumbles, and Stumbles

The Biden age issue was further compounded by Biden. It was nothing he did, said, or any action of his. It was the incessant focus by much of the media on a real or alleged Biden gaffe, a slip of the tongue, or a mixed-up date or fact. Even worse, there was the continued lookout for a trip, stumble, or seeming walking problem. This was magnified, blown up, and relentlessly finger-pointed at by many in the media.

A near textbook example of this was Biden's trip on stage while handing out diplomas at the Air Force Academy graduation in June 2023. That was the hot topic all day long on nearly all the network channels at the time. It came complete with generous reruns of the trip.

A partly chagrined, partly amused Biden had to quickly respond to the standard inference that the trip was due to age. "I got sandbagged," he said. He meant that literally. There were two sandbags placed inconspicuously on the stage, and Biden stumbled against one of them. A White House spokesperson quickly assured that, "He's fine." That assurance was far from convincing to a legion of nervous Democrats.

No matter how much energy and vigor Biden displayed in public appearances, it did not cancel out any gaffe or stumble that Biden foes, and much of the media, was obsessed with harping on. A September 2023, a *Forbes* magazine report was by then typical. It meticulously itemized for that month alone Biden's missteps, in some cases literally. The magazine listed these fumbles:

- Biden slipped as he deboarded Air Force One on a jaunt to Michigan.

- Biden's staff revealed that it was taking measures to prevent his tripping and even falling.

- Biden now wore tennis shoes and had been working with a physical therapist for over two years to better control his balance.

- Biden had a memory lapse during an address about where he was during the 9/11 terror attack

- Biden joked at a press conference during a visit to Hanoi that he was going to bed. He made the joke after he gave a convoluted, jumbled answer to a press question.

- Biden walked out of the East Room of the White House during a ceremony to honor a Vietnam war veteran. A White House spokesperson when questioned about it said that he left to limit his possible exposure to COVID.

Forbes went on to tick off a litany of Biden stumbles, literally and figuratively, that stretched back through 2023.

*****

Another point to the question of Biden's age and his ability to do the presidential job was given almost no attention. Ironically, that point came from an unlikely source, Trump. When asked in an interview about Biden's age, Trump didn't hesitate: "He's not too old." But this was not altruism or political generosity on Trump's part. He had an ulterior motive. He quickly added that it was not his age, but his competency: "He's grossly incompetent." Trump noted that there were many instances of aged world leaders who performed ably and even superbly as national and world leaders.

Trump had yet another ulterior motive in downplaying Biden's age as an issue. He was only three years younger than him, and he didn't want to look over his shoulder and worry that someone just might start slapping the "he's too old" label on him. More than a few GOP insiders and some of the public continued to do just that.

One was former Trump White House official Alyssa Farah Griffin. During a *CNN* panel discussion in December 2023 at a Trump campaign rally in Iowa, she expressed shock over Trump's delivery on and command of the issues. She said he lacked "sharpness." She claimed that he seemed confused and badly bungled his promise to again try to dump Obamacare. "There's a lack of sharpness in what he's saying and a lack of kind of clarity—complete inconsistencies."

From the moment he took office in 2020, the talk was that Biden was too old for a second term. Biden seemingly partially fed into this notion in reported comments he made about a second term during the campaign. The source for this was several Biden campaign advisors who gave an interview in December 2019. They gave the impression, allegedly based on conversations with Biden, that he would only serve one term. The reason was his advancing age.

"If Biden is elected," said one adviser, "he's going to be eighty-two years old in four years and he won't be running for reelection." Another adviser reportedly said: "He's going into this thinking, 'I want to find a running mate I can turn things over to after four years, but if that's not possible or doesn't happen then I'll run for reelection.' But he's not going to publicly make a one-term pledge."

While that seemed to scotch any notion that Biden was seriously considering limiting his White House tenure if elected to one term, it still provided much fodder for the media to continue its drumbeat focus on Biden's age. *Forbes* quickly cited an AP report from October 2019 in which Biden reportedly said that he would not publicly commit to running for a second term at that juncture.

"I feel good and all I can say is, watch me, you'll see," he told the AP at the time. "It doesn't mean I would run a second term. I'm not going to make that judgment at this moment."

*****

After his election in 2020, the discussion of his possibly being a one-term-and-done president stepped up. The inference was that he would gracefully turn the 2024 Democratic presidential election reins over to a younger person. Biden ended all the talk and speculation when he announced in April 2023 that he was running again.

His supporters quickly brushed aside the talk that he was not up to the job. Cedric Richmond, a former senior White House advisor, was emphatic that he was "handling a grueling schedule," sometimes requiring ten- and fourteen-hour days and reading a fat briefing book each night to prepare for the next day.

Richmond further added, "In meetings, he's asking detailed questions, thorough questions, because he's already read the briefing material. You have to be prepared when you meet with him. And he's going to quiz you on what's there: How does it affect the American people? The average person? How does it move the agenda forward? Are there any consequences? What kind of studies have been done?"

Biden confidently told an interviewer who asked about his fitness, "Read the polls, Jack. You guys are all the same. That poll showed that 92% of Democrats, if I ran, would vote for me." He referred, of course, to a 2024 repeat show-down with Trump. However, that still didn't silence the critics.

At the National Governors Association's winter meeting in February 2023, the talk was incessant about Biden's age as a possible political liability. More than one top Democratic governor worried that Biden would not be able to do much campaigning. Why, again, because of his age? This was tantamount to saying he was an old broken-down old mule ready to be put out to pasture.

Another top Democrat tried yet another approach. He went to Biden's wife Jill, and brashly suggested that maybe her husband should consider his presidency a one-term victory of accomplishment, take a victory lap, and then quietly withdraw from the 2024 presidential derby.

Still others took a backhand approach to Biden's fitness and stamina. They banked on limiting the number of presidential debates, preferably to only one, that Biden would have to engage in. By then it was far too late to switch Democratic presidential horses. And even more compelling, the governors, at least publicly, were unanimous that Biden was the only Democrat who could win.

Ohio Democratic congresswoman Joyce Beatty firmly noted, "He's the president. And right now, he says he's going to be our candidate. And people will fall in line because he can win the general election." She punctuated the point: "Biden is the guy that can beat Trump."

She spoke what was a realistic truth to some. But to others, it was a bitter truth.

5

Reagan Got the "Too Old" Knock, Too

"How could you do a good job at your age?" No, the question wasn't directed to Biden. It was asked repeatedly of then GOP presidential candidate Ronald Reagan. One month after he took office in January, 1981, he turned seventy. That made him the oldest man, at that time, to ever hold the presidency.

It wasn't just many in the press who were asking this question. Many members of the public, some elected officials, and assorted political pundits all questioned Reagan's health, fitness, and stamina at seventy. Many gerontologists were also asked what Reagan's seemingly advanced age meant for the presidency and, by extension, the country.

Most agreed with Reagan that age should not be the prime factor in assessing a president's competency for the office. This was the near-consensus view on the age issue that prevailed during the Reagan administration. "Age has always been a topic of discussion in presidential politics. While concerns about a candidate's physical and cognitive health are valid, it is crucial to evaluate candidates holistically, considering their experience, leadership abilities, and policy proposals," one medical expert concluded. "Ronald Reagan's presidency provides a historical reference point for analyzing the impact of age on presidential performance. Ultimately, age should not be the sole determining factor in assessing a candidate's fitness for the highest office in the United States."

Reagan answered the age doubters by making sure he was shown in abundant photo ops riding horses and doing manual labor outdoors. The critics mostly bought the story of Reagan's fitness. The word during his presidency was that he always looked and seemed younger than his age. But not everyone was convinced that his age wasn't a liability.

Even after Reagan underwent colon cancer surgery in July 1985, many of the accounts of the surgery and his recovery mentioned his age. Reagan again attempted to squash the speculation about his health and age. He put a cheery face on his recovery: "Well, I'm glad that's all out." He also said that he "planned to live a long time." Reagan, seventy-four, was then the nation's oldest serving president.

But that wasn't enough. One publication was so concerned with his age that it asked Reagan's former Attorney General Ed Meese about it:

Meese: He would usually finish work around five to six, go back to the quarters, and work out for forty-five minutes to an hour. He had a treadmill and a weight-lifting machine while he watched the evening news.

Baroch: You were on the campaign with him in the 1980s. Did you ever see him flagging at all?

Meese: No, not really. I think one of the things was, when he got up in front of an audience, he was on. That stimulated him.

*****

Still, the notion that Reagan was too old for the presidency was never totally dispelled. Reagan knew it and again attempted to put an upbeat face on the recovery period after his surgery for colon cancer. He defied the advice of his physicians and was back riding horses. He defiantly told all who cautioned him to take things easier, "'I'm not slowing down. Nothing is going to slow me down."

Reagan's bravado though wasn't enough to stop the whispers and concern about his age. When he was under intense scrutiny in 1987 for his role in the Iran-Contra scandal, a popular joke that made the rounds among Washington insiders was the question, "What did President Reagan forget and when did he forget it?" Reagan by then was seventy-five.

At that point, Reagan had been in office for more than six years. That should have been more than ample time to determine if age had slowed him down or impaired his decision-making. Yet the Iran-Contra dig at Reagan's age was another reminder that his vigorous work schedule did not satisfy the ageists. He was quietly ridiculed during the 1984 reelection campaign for occasionally mangling or forgetting facts and names.

The debate on the issue turned red hot following his performance in his first debate in 1984 with his Democratic rival Walter Mondale. It was called "halting," "ineffective," "garbled," and worse.

Few shirked this time from openly blaming his performance on his age. A worried Reagan adviser who declined to be identified observed: "It's the one issue that could change the course of this campaign. We don't think it will, but the potential is now there." Though Reagan was still comfortably ahead of Mondale in the polls, his overall rating dropped three percent afterward.

Democrats, who until that point had gingerly tipped around the age issue, now pounced. California Democrat Tony Coelho, chair of the Democratic Congressional Campaign Committee, said that Reagan "looked old and acted old." Other Democrats followed suit with the "too old" line about Reagan.

Reagan again didn't back away from the issue and as in the past used a physical fitness analogy in his retort. At a press conference he carped, "I'll challenge him to an arm-wrestle any time," in an apparent reference to Mondale, aged fifty-six.

Friendly medical experts backed Reagan with a ready-made but plausible excuse to explain his poor performance. "In general, his possible shortcomings, if there were any, during the debate were probably as attributable to physical fatigue as to any shortcomings of the mental processes," one expert noted. "But when people get physically tired, they become mentally tired as well."

Mondale wisely stayed detached from making Reagan's age an issue, fearing a backlash. A senior adviser said: "No. We won't go near it—and we don't have to. It's out there right now and people will decide for themselves how big a factor it is."

Ironically, it wasn't the first time that Reagan had been ripped on his advancing age. The first attack came not from a Democratic rival but a GOP presidential rival. In that case, it was his eventual VP pick, George H.W. Bush. He referenced Reagan's age during their primary battles in 1980 and left dangling the question of whether that rendered him problematic in winning the presidency.

*****

The critics were especially on the lookout to see if Reagan exhibited any of the early signs of dementia. During his presidential years, the general view was that there were no signs.

However, a quarter century later, that abruptly changed. Reagan's namesake son, Ronald Reagan Jr., in a bombshell book, *My Father at 100*, published in 2011, claimed that his father "may have shown signs of Alzheimer's disease as early as three years into his first term." Reagan Jr. was quickly taken to task for this assertion by his brother Michael and other Reagan acolytes. Yet, other Reagan watchers chimed in with their own recollections of alleged Reagan fumbles and seeming mental lapses during their close encounters with him.

Just why was this so important decades after Reagan had left office and died? Said one mental health expert, "It's critical to ask whether the president of the United States was mentally impaired toward the end of his term in office. The implications of that inquiry extend far beyond a family feud. They spotlight the many other, far less attractive policy decisions, both at home and abroad, that Reagan authorized and initiated." That was a valid point about competency and the presidency. But the real issue still centered on the tie to age.

The fact that Reagan would be near eighty when he left office after a second term did not quiet the age watchers. That included, not surprisingly, various top medical practitioners who observed and commented on Reagan's performance in office.

Most agreed with Richard Restak, a leading Washington neurologist, and author of *The Brain*. His assessment, "When we consider the case of Ronald Reagan, America's foremost septuagenarian, we have to put him into context. Has he changed? The criticism is made that his communications are low in specific information and high in anecdotes.

"But they have been for years. This, apparently, is his style. Or, some say, he misses the point of a question at press conferences. Since his days as an actor, he has always done better when working from a script. Briefed on what to say beforehand, he does fine. Even in instances where he seems to stray from the point, he generally comes back to it, as opposed to the 'circumstantiality' of the senile person who wanders from the point and never returns."

"Comes back to it" was an apt description of Reagan in his second debate with Mondale at the Municipal Auditorium in Kansas City, Missouri in October, 1984. He of course made the famous retort, "I want you to know that also I will not make age an issue of this campaign. I am not going to exploit, for political purposes, my opponent's youth, and inexperience. If I still have time, I might add, Mr. Trehwitt, I might add that it was Seneca, or it was Cicero, I don't know which, that said, 'If it was not for the elders correcting the mistakes of the young, there would be no state.'"

Then he went further and explained that his poor performance in his first debate had nothing to do with age, but rather to overpreparation on the part of his staff. Reagan again muted the age issue and, in the process, got a big bump-up in the polls after the debate.

The ultimate retort to the age critics was victory. He crushed Mondale in the election. He won forty-nine of the fifty states. He and Nixon were the only presidential candidates in American presidential election history to accomplish that feat. While that may have buried the age issue as an issue regarding Reagan, it did not end it for another presidential candidate.

6

McCain Got the "Too Old" Knock, Too

"I've served with seven presidents. When they come in, they all make mistakes. They all get older. This one guy running is about as old as me. Let me tell you something, it's no old man's job."

Pennsylvania Congressman John Murtha got raucous applause and a lot of laughs from the audience at the AFL-CIO's Building Trades National Legislative Conference in April, 2008 when he cracked jokes about the age of 2008 GOP Presidential candidate John McCain.

Murtha could poke fun at McCain's advanced age because he was right up there with him age-wise. In fact, at seventy-five, he was four years older than McCain. He also could take great license with age at McCain's expense because he was a Democrat and McCain was a Republican. There was more than a little political partisanship at work here. He was introducing then-New York Senator Hillary Clinton to the rock-solid Democratic-leaning union bigwigs.

Yet, Murtha's dig at McCain as being "too old" fit neatly into one of the major narratives about the 2008 presidential election. That was whether McCain at age seventy-two years would be up to handling the stress and rigors of the presidency if elected. Murtha flatly said no. Others said or privately thought so, too. McCain, if he won, would have topped Reagan as the oldest man ever to occupy the Oval Office.

McCain, as with Reagan and years later Biden, sought to turn the tables on the age detractors with levity when confronted with the "too old" to be president charge. On one occasion, he faked to reporters that he was falling asleep. He quickly snapped to and challenged, "Watch me campaign. We keep a heavier schedule. We campaign harder. People will judge me by my performance. I am confident that my energy, my intellect, my experience, and my judgment is what American people will—hopefully, that they will view me as qualified to be president of the United States." As for Murtha's ageist put-down, he had only two words to describe them: "nonsense attacks."

*****

Still, a quarter century after Reagan left office, the too old to be president issue was back on the table. McCain's opponent during the 2008 presidential campaign was the decades younger and, compounding the age issue, high schoolish-looking Barack Obama.

The marked contrast between the two age-wise cropped up repeatedly during the campaign. It was inevitable, even if McCain was not seventy-two at the start of the campaign. The age gap was the largest in American history between two presidential candidates. A *Newsweek* editorial on the McCain-Obama matchup capsulized how the massive age gap between the two candidates would play out in how each would come at the other.

"The contrast is already stark. Obama is 46 and looks 40; McCain is 71 and looks closer to 80, though he's got more energy than someone half his age. Their matchup would represent the largest age gap between major- party presidential candidates in American history. The campaign would pit change vs. experience, fresh vs. tested, green vs. gray. Once their niceties about one's heroism and the other's inspiration are dispensed with, Obama would try to make the Arizona senator look like a hypocritical, clueless, and warlike geezer, while McCain would suggest that the Illinois senator is a naive, liberal, and dreamy kid."

To drive home the "too old" issue with McCain, another reporter ticked off a list of products such as computers, credit cards, and automatic transmissions on cars that did not exist when McCain was born. Another pointed out that McCain would be far too old to qualify as an Air Force pilot which was what he had been and gained military fame as.

While a majority in polls did not say McCain was too old to assume office, a significant minority did. Not surprisingly, many of those who did voice reservations about McCain's age were themselves somewhat long in the tooth age-wise. One seventy-plus-year-old voter typified that sentiment, saying, "Sure, people live to be ninety, but you are not as sharp. I'm not as sharp as I was ten years ago, and I'm sure (McCain) isn't either—even though he wouldn't admit it."

In an *AP-Yahoo News* poll in July, 2008, twenty percent of the respondents said that "too old" described McCain "very well." Another thirty-eight percent of respondents said "too old" described McCain somewhat or very well.

*****

An issue that underlaid much of the debate and concern about McCain landing in the Oval Office was not just his fitness and stamina for the job, but whether he'd even be alive to finish his term or terms. This was largely a false fear. In 2008, the normal life expectancy for someone seventy years old was that they'd live another fifteen years. If the life expectancy demographic held up, McCain would not only finish a possible second term but would be around for many years afterwards to lecture and write about his White House years.

Democratic Party strategist Garry South didn't buy that assessment about McCain's chances of survival if elected. "McCain, of course, has experienced four bouts of potentially deadly malignant melanoma, the latest in 2002, and has had untold other, less-serious skin cancers excised," noted South. "Compared with the general population, melanoma patients have a far higher risk of developing melanoma in the future. Medical experts also say men have a lower melanoma survival rate than women. And no one's immune system at 72 is as strong as at 42 or 52."

Eight years earlier, in 2008, McCain had a lesion removed. However, since that time he had complete checkup exams every few months to guard against any reoccurrence. To further silence the doubters, McCain authorized the release of more than one thousand pages of his medical exam reports from 2000 to 2008. He got a clean bill of health. "I do not see any worrisome lesions," Dr. Suzanne Connolly of the Mayo Clinic noted following an exam he took six months before the November presidential election.

Inevitably the debate over McCain's age drew in medical experts, "As a clinician, I look at whether they appear to be robust, whether their sentences flow, whether their thoughts connect, whether they are easily distractible," said David Reuben, chief of geriatrics at UCLA's David Geffen School of Medicine. "McCain appears to be quite robust."

*****

The pushback to the "too old" to be president, from a candidate such as Reagan, McCain, or Biden, was that they had a vast storehouse of experience to draw on. One much younger voter agreed in discussing the McCain presidential candidacy, "I figure he's a very experienced man.

We've had presidents who were up there in age before." McCain underscored that when he quipped, "I'm older than dirt and have more scars than Frankenstein, but I've learned a few things along the way."

McCain played hard on that during the campaign, essentially using his experience over Obama as another way to stand the age question on its head. Some in the media were quick to pick up on that.

There was a spate of articles that claimed that the election was about change (Obama) versus experience (McCain). A May 2008, *Gallup* poll delved deep into the issues surrounding the voter perception of McCain's experience versus Obama. Voters were nearly matched percentage-wise between those who gave the edge to McCain on experience and those who gave the edge to Obama on his change pitch.

Those who leaned toward McCain ticked off his war record and military service, his leadership abilities, and that he was conservative. Age was not mentioned. Gallup concluded, "McCain supporters have developed more specific explanations for their support based on their candidate's issue positions and personal characteristics than is the case for Obama supporters."

Age, though now mentioned, worked in McCain's favor. He had been in public office for decades. He was a known quantity. He appeared steady on the issues. This made him almost a wise father figure who could be depended on to maintain a firm hand on the ship of state as opposed to the youngish Obama, a relative newcomer to politics on the national scene.

*****

There was yet another seemingly age-related concern that McCain had to weather, and in the process continually assure and reassure voters it would not be an issue if he was elected. That was his mental well-being.

Studies were cited that made this more worrisome. They showed that more than twenty percent of Americans over age seventy-one did have some fall-off in their mental capacity, primarily in memory loss. Another thirty-five percent of seventy-plus Americans had a higher rate of what were gingerly branded as "neural deficits."

Those deficits supposedly were the prime cause of verbal slips, gaffes, confusion, and poor decision-making. McCain was watched hawk-like during the campaign for any sign of a "neural deficit." Many wondered out loud whether his malaprops were a sign of mental slippage.

In a span of a few weeks during the campaign, McCain got things wrong about where Iraq was located, called then-former President Vladimir Putin, the Russian president, and referred to Czechoslovakia even after it had split into two countries as though it still was one country. Each of these was endlessly pointed to by some as proof that McCain was losing it.

Neurologists seemed to confirm this possibility when their studies showed that memory loss can lead people to substitute incorrect information. They had a somewhat medically ominous term they attached to this confusion: "confabulation." Inquiring reporters were quick to note that McCain had not had any mental aptitude tests or evaluations in years. The unstated conclusion of the age detractors was the possible danger of a man who might hold the most powerful political position in the world, the American presidency, having a failing mind.

The jury, though, for many medical experts was still out: "I've been studying cognitive aging for 30 years, and it is the case that the 70-year-olds in our research now are cognitively younger than those we studied 20 years ago," said Karlene Ball, Director University of Alabama-Birmingham's Roybal Center for Research on Applied Gerontology. "But," she cautioned, "there is a downward slope in memory as a function of age, though there are enormous individual differences."

McCain shrugged this off. His strategy, beyond continually citing his steady and productive work record, was to defuse the talk with sly humor that mostly played along with the age stereotypes. He'd just come across as the proverbial old cranky guy and hope that audiences laughed along rather than jeered.

So, when a seven-year-old confronted McCain in New Hampshire the year before the election about his age, he shot back, "Thanks for the question, you little jerk." The audience and presumably the seven-year-old took it in good humor and laughed along.

During the campaign, Obama and top Democrats were careful not to give McCain any ammunition by openly making an issue of his age. When asked directly about

McCain's age, Obama brusquely told reporters, "I don't think so. Senator McCain is healthy, he is campaigning actively all across the country, his doctors have given him a clean bill of health, I don't think it should be an issue in the campaign."

However, there were other ways to continually remind voters about his age and keep clean hands while doing it. In September 2008, the Obama campaign took out an attack ad. It hammered McCain for not using email. The ad came complete with pictures of a misshapen cordless phone and a Rubik's Cube. The imagery was deliberately confounding and confusing. The idea was to convey the notion that McCain, in not being tech-savvy, belonged to another time in America. The ad drew swift and harsh outrage. It was ripped as tasteless and immature.

Another subtle if not outright sneaky way to raise voter doubts about McCain's age was not to harp on him being "too old," but rather to compare and contrast him with the tens of millions who are younger than him. A few websites popped up that seemingly poked fun at McCain's age by not only ticking off the things that weren't around when McCain was young but even mentioning Obama's parent's age. They would have been the same age as McCain.

A video released by the Democratic consulting firm The Organizing Group, dubbed "McAncient," featured a crude-if-occasionally-clever song with lines like "He's older than his wife, a little younger than his mama/He's old enough to be one and a half Barack Obamas." The creators also maintained their own "Younger Than McCain" site.

One media outlet even tossed in McCain's advocacy for high- definition television to skewer him as too old. It noted that as this exposed his "[w]rinkles, blotches, liver spots, scarry tissue to the masses, it may be impossible to keep the issue below the radar until Election Day."

*****

McCain ignored these types of jibes. He continued to punch back with humor. In an appearance on *Saturday Night Live*, he cracked, "I ask you, what should we be looking for in our next president? Certainly, someone who is very, very, very old. I have the courage, the wisdom, the experience, and, most importantly, the oldness necessary. The oldness it takes to protect America, to honor her, love her, and tell her about what cute things the cat did."

In May 2008, Obama did tell an interviewer that McCain had "lost his bearings" in pursuing the Republican nomination. He didn't elaborate. But the seed had been planted. Massachusetts Democratic Senator John Kerry used similar code language when he called McCain "unbelievably out of touch" and said that he "confuses history" on the Iraq conflict. Obama's top foreign policy advisor Susan Rice latched onto the code word "confusing." She warned that he had a "pattern of confusing the basic facts and reality that pertain to Iraq."

McCain was not fooled. He lambasted their characterization of him as nothing more than a sneaky way to take a shot at him with voters that he was too old. The Obama camp called the charge that they were promoting ageism as "unfair" and "ridiculous."

McCain ultimately lost the 2008 presidential election to Obama. But the loss had nothing to do with age and everything to do with voters desperately wanting a change.

Obama made his hope and change theme the signature mark and promise of his campaign. The voters bought that and nothing else.

Apart from the age issue, Biden would almost certainly win or lose in 2024, as McCain lost and Reagan won, on issues that were far removed from the age question. Those issues were the usual voter concerns. They were jobs, the economy, inflation, foreign policy handling, legislative accomplishments, and most critically, whether voters perceived things—meaning the country's future—would be better or worse during a Biden second term. Those were ageless issues in any and every presidential campaign.

7

It's Not Just Biden—
US Politicians Are Old

How old were the Democrats running in the 2024 election?

- Joe Biden: 80

- Marianne Williamson: 71

- Robert F. Kennedy, Jr: 69

How old were the Republicans running in the 2024 election?

- Donald Trump: 77

True, there were a slew of much younger Republicans and a couple of Democrats who were running or expressed interest in a presidential run in 2024. However, as the names of the aged 2024 presidential candidates showed, it wasn't just Biden and Trump that fed the relentless chatter and complaints that American elected officials and would-be elected officials were old, if not too old to be running the ship of state.

Headlines in publications pronounced that "The Democratic Party has an age problem," "Washington is run by old people," and "They're 80 plus and in charge and they aren't going away." There would be many more headlines and articles that obsessed over Biden's age and the aging of other elected officials throughout the 2024 presidential race. GOP presidential candidate Nikki Haley grabbed the biggest headline on Capitol Hill's aging issue when she referred to the U.S. Senate as America's "most privileged nursing home."

The issue of age was now firmly rammed into the political debate about how old was too old for politicians to be holding elected office. Much of the talk about age was aimed at not just Biden, but also at other Democrats. The prime target of the age question for a time was California Democratic Senator Dianne Feinstein.

In 2022, she was nearing age ninety. She'd served in the Senate for decades. She was chronically ill and often missed sessions or showed signs of mental lapses. Many Democrats railed that she was a political liability for the party. They clamored for her to step down. California Democratic congressperson Ro Khanna was typical of this view. "It's time for @SenFeinstein to resign. We need to put the country ahead of personal loyalty. While she has had a lifetime of public service, it is obvious she can no longer fulfill her duties. Not speaking out undermines our credibility as elected representatives of the people."

Feinstein refused to step down. In a statement in March 2023, she defiantly said, "I intend to return as soon as possible once my medical team advises that it's safe for me to travel. In the meantime, I remain committed to the job and will continue to work from home in San Francisco."

This only increased the ire in many quarters. It took death to finally pry her seat from her. She died at age ninety in September 2023, still refusing to relinquish her seat.

Feinstein was a convenient official to target on the age issue. She underscored the problem, as many saw it, of too many older people staying in office for far too long. Meanwhile, they remained tightly in command of running the government.

*****

By the 2020 presidential election, the average Democratic congressperson or senator was aged sixty-plus. The average age for their Republican counterparts was fifty-seven. In the decade before the election, the age of the top Republican and Democratic elected officials had steadily crept upward. The too-old issue repeatedly drew comment and even bitterness, especially when it came to the Democratic party's congressional leadership.

In 2020, the top three House Democratic leaders were in their late seventies and fast closing in on age eighty. Among them was Minority and later Majority House leader Nancy Pelosi. She had turned age eighty.

Predictably, many younger Democrats openly demanded that Pelosi and the other septuagenarians and octogenarians turn over the reins of leadership to younger Democrats. "There comes a time when you need to pass that torch," noted Linda Sanchez, the vice chair of the House Democratic Caucus. "I think it's time."

By the time Sanchez made her demand, Pelosi had held a firm grip on the House Democratic leadership for more than two decades. Eventually, Pelosi bowed to the inevitable and stepped down in 2022. But her decision had less to do with her age and the calls for her to step aside. It had much to do with the fact that the GOP had taken back control of the

House in the 2022 midterm elections. Pelosi was now out as House Majority Leader anyway.

GOP leaders didn't escape the intense glare of age either. Long-time Senate Minority Leader Mitch McConnell drew a mix of laughter, partisan ridicule, and sympathy when he appeared to freeze in mid-sentence at a press event in Covington, Kentucky, in August 2023. McConnell was asked the obviously age-tinged question of whether he would run again for reelection in 2026.

His mid-sentence freeze was not just a pause but lasted more than thirty seconds. That might have drawn scant notice and could have been chalked up to a politician being politically coy about his future election plans. However, aides had to prompt McConnell to answer. Then a staff member had to repeat to him two more questions that reporters had asked.

McConnell's freeze and seeming memory lapse might have been passed off as just a momentary flub—except it was not the first time it happened. The month before McConnell froze for twenty seconds, again in mid-sentence during a press conference. He was quickly hustled from the press conference by a slew of other Republican senators.

This triggered a brief flurry of concern by GOP senators. There was talk of having a "special conference" to hash out whether it might be time to think about another GOP Senate leader to replace McConnell. That was not likely to happen. Like Pelosi, McConnell held a tight grip on the top GOP Senate leadership post.

The McConnell freeze also had repercussions for Biden. Both were roughly the same age. Some in the GOP instantly saw this and moved quickly once more to remind the public of his age vulnerability.

"I think that the Mitch McConnell situation hurts Joe Biden more than it hurts the Republican Party," noted Republican pollster and Bellwether Research president Christine Matthews. "So, when you see somebody like Mitch McConnell freezing up, having these problems, I think it ... puts pressure on [Mr. Biden] to address the age issue."

Despite his dismissal of age as an issue in the campaign, Trump also couldn't resist getting in his digs at Biden. In a social media post, he made fun of Biden calling him "one of the oldest 79s in history" and claiming that he'd be hard-pressed to lift a beach chair.

This was partisan political disingenuousness, to say the least. Biden had constantly joked, made references to, and pushed back on the age issue every chance he got. When he turned eighty, in a radio interview he cracked, "I can't even say that number, eighty... I no more feel that than I'd get out from behind this desk and fly."

He laughingly told an audience at a Black History Month event in February 2022, "I look back on my career of 280 years." He delivered a variation of this gag line at the Air Force Academy graduation ceremony in June 2022: "When I was graduating from high school 300 years ago, I applied to the Naval Academy."

*****

At the close of 2023, Feinstein, Biden, Pelosi, and McConnell, just by being the leading and most visible names in American political circles for decades, continually assured that the age issue would stay front and center in the media and public opinion. The question always was "when was it too old to be elected and hold office?" It also continually raised the issue of how effective an elected official could be who had passed the seventy-year mark.

More than a few elected officials had served in the Senate in their eighties and even nineties. Before the flap over Biden's age, their advanced age was an issue that largely passed under the radar for the media as well as the public. The older elected officials were routinely in most cases easily reelected term after term.

If their constituents were satisfied with their performance, there seemed to be no reason to raise any doubt or concern about them being too old to hold the office. There was rarely any demand made that they step down because of their age. "There is a tremendous incumbency," observed Nathan Gonzales, the editor of *Inside Elections*. "If the incumbent decides to run again, then it is very difficult for anyone of any age to knock them off."

However, age and the length of time served in the Senate or House did weigh heavily on some long-serving elected officials. Increasingly, more of them chose not to seek reelection. But it was their call, not that of the party or the voters.

Before Biden's election, the advancing age of the House and Senate leadership was not a dominant public issue for another reason. Americans in general were getting older.

They were living longer, staying healthier, and in many cases were active and retained much of their vigor.

So having an aged seventy-plus senator or House member merely reflected the changing age demographic of America. A seventy-year-plus senator or House elected official, while not quite the norm age-wise for an office holder, was no longer an anomaly either. That certainly was the case for McConnell even after he seemed to flub a reporter's question that some took as showing his age.

*****

The question of aging politicians running the government for so long seemed to require an explanation for younger persons, particularly since the median age in America was under age forty in 2020. The term that younger persons often heard to describe the country's political leadership was "gerontocracy."

The term was defined as "government by the elderly." The comparison was made to the Vatican, the Iranian leadership, and the old men who ran the show in the old Soviet Union for decades. The top-heavy number of older men and women who ran government in the U.S. now as opposed to the past seemed to mirror the pattern in these places.

What mystified many about the refusal of so many aged American elected officials to go quietly into retirement was that they were all well-heeled financially, had full government pensions and medical benefits, and could lead very comfortable lives outside of the political arena. This sharply contrasted with the standard reason for delaying retirement, namely, that the person needed the money and couldn't afford to stop working.

The explanation for older politicians staying on was much simpler. For them it was the sense of duty, the feeling of accomplishment, the allure of holding an office, the attention and glitter of being an elected official, and the sense of importance. Most importantly, many were hopelessly smitten with the intoxication of holding and exercising power. These were all powerful motivating factors that made it nearly impossible for most aging politicians to step down.

Said one political analyst, "In the political world, their interest is often about power as well. These are the types who think: Why wouldn't I want to keep casting deciding votes in a closely divided House or Senate, or keep giving speeches and flying around on *Air Force One* as president, or telling myself I'm saving democracy? It's easy to see why so few of them want to walk away."

*****

It was no surprise then that every call and effort to impose age limits on elected officials, especially federal officials, got nowhere over the years. To skirt this barrier and put some kind of check in place to ensure that aged officeholders were up to the job, there were calls for mandatory mental competency tests for elected officials.

Under this proposal, a failure to pass such a test wouldn't automatically disqualify an official from office. However, it would provide some gauge as to the continued ability of that official to do the job. Polls showed that a majority of Americans favored such a proposal.

The proposal made good copy and sounded like something that might help determine whether aging elected officials were still cognitively fit to do the job. However, medical experts warned that such tests wouldn't work for the simple fact that there were no reliable, one-size-fits-all cognitive tests to determine mental fitness.

One expert noted, "The American military for many years has used a test to predict how somebody would fare in different professions. And you know, that does OK. But to predict something as complex as being a U.S. senator or a president of a major country, I know of no such tests." He also observed, "As we get older, memory tends to decline to some degree, how quickly we can respond tends to decline, but there are huge individual differences."

Medical experts even coined the term "super-agers" to describe those who don't fit the stereotype of an aged person who is enfeebled, doddering, and slipping fast cognitively. A 2020 article in the *Journal on Active Aging* proclaimed that Biden and Trump likely were super-agers because they appeared to "maintain their mental and physical functioning into late life and tend to live longer than the average person their age."

In any case, any proposal that required aging elected officials to take mental competency tests, as with age limit proposals, would almost certainly have been dead on arrival. No elected official came close to echoing the call President John F. Kennedy made in 1961 to pass the torch of leadership to a new generation of Americans.

Americans would have to take some comfort in the often-repeated admonition that a healthy seventy-plus person, given the vast improvement in medical and health advances and awareness, could have the vigor of someone a decade or more younger. If so, the new norm in 2024 was that a senior citizen American politician would and could run the political show in the country for years to come.

The debate over an age limit would not likely go away. The question as one analyst asked, "Should there be maximum limits, too? This question remains open." However, his answer was the one that would always likely stand: "In a democracy, we the people decide by voting."

8

Should There Be an Age Limit on Politicians?

In August 2022, *CBS News/YouGov* conducted a survey. The topic was "Should there be an age limit on politicians?" It was a first. And almost certainly it was prompted by the relentless controversy and debate over Biden's age, and indeed the aging of more than a few other top elected officials. Quite a few.

In Congress in 2022 the average age of congresspersons was the highest in two decades. Some of them, such as Senate Minority Leader McConnell, had embarrassing moments of freezes, stumbles, and seeming disorientation. In short, that was tantamount to a public meltdown.

Given the intense media and public focus on the age issue, there was little surprise in the survey's findings. The overwhelming majority of Americans irrespective of their political affiliation—Republican, Democrat, Independent—resoundingly said "yes" there should be a *maximum* age limit for elected officials. Put more starkly, most Americans felt that aging politicians should be given a graceful exit from office when they reached whatever the proscribed maximum age set.

There was more. The age maximum limit cut across all age demographics. Both young and old respondents agreed on the need for a limit and that political office holding should be best left to younger people. In line with that sentiment, many older people said they too felt that ripe-old-age politicians only made politics worse.

Interestingly, a greater majority of seniors than young people aged eighteen to twenty-nine said that there should be age limitations. One of them was former President Jimmy Carter, who at the time of the survey was nearing the age one-hundred-year mark. Age seventy was the age most agreed on for elected officials and would-be elected officials to gracefully step aside.

*****

The debate over an age limit for politicians in some ways mirrored the off-again, on-again debate over term limits for elected officials. There are none for congresspersons.

Proposals for congressional term limits were introduced first in the 1990s. At that time, nearly two dozen states had enacted term limit requirements on elected officials at the state and local levels. In 1994, then-House Speaker Newt Gingrich liked the idea. A majority of House members backed a Constitutional amendment that would have set a term for a legislator at twelve years. It would have meant six two-year terms for House members and two six-year terms for senators.

The SCOTUS though scotched any potential momentum for such an amendment when it ruled against states slapping stricter limits on their state's representatives than federal term limits. Several GOP representatives openly tied term limits to a move to oust aging members.

Even without the SCOTUS ruling, the blunt truth was that term limits got no political traction. The argument was always that having a term limit would be detrimental to their constituents since they would lose the clout that seasoned elected officials brought to bear with their experience and vital legislative contacts.

That was not the argument of opponents of age limitations. Rather an age limitation was blatant discrimination and illegal. They also cited packs of medical experts and scientists who repeatedly pointed out that Americans were living longer and living healthier than ever—and that there was no evidence that the mental acuity of older Americans automatically plunged with advancing age.

"One of the arguments against the term limits is that there is a distinction between people *thinking* [politicians] shouldn't serve too long and creating laws enshrining those beliefs," observed Nick Beauchamp, assistant professor of political science at Northeastern. His solution, rather than trying to impose an artificial age standard, was to simply vote them out. He was a bit more diplomatic in calling for the addressing of the issue through "normal democratic voting and persuasion."

That was by no means a given. Vermont Democratic Senator Bernie Sanders at age eighty was the oldest candidate in the race for president in 2016 and again in 2020. This inevitably prompted the cry from some that he was too old to be running. CNN's Anderson Cooper didn't mince any words on the issue.

In a Democratic presidential candidate's town hall discussion in February 2016, Cooper asked Sanders if his age could be an issue, since if elected and he served two terms he would be eighty-three at the end of his second term. Sanders quickly and sharply retorted, "Let's not be ageist." Cooper wisely dropped the issue. Wisely, because Sanders proved himself right in his response. He generated far more enthusiasm and support from younger people, much younger people, than any of the other, younger candidate. Quipped one pundit, "Young people don't seem to care that Sanders was born before Pearl Harbor."

The "when is too old" debate didn't just roil controversy over elected officials staying on well past their prime. It roiled the judiciary. Age limitations advocates zeroed in on the aging and ailing Ruth Bader Ginsberg who resisted all calls for her to step down from the SCOTUS before her death in September 2020.

In this case, the age proponents wanted both age and term limit requirements slapped on the SCOTUS and federal judges. There was no chance of that happening. With Ginsberg's death, the issue largely passed for the time. There was no mandatory age requirement for federal judges. Nor was there any indication during the 2024 presidential year that there would be.

However, that was not the case with the states. In 2024 more than two dozen states and the District of Columbia had mandatory retirement ages for their judges. The age limits ranged from seventy to seventy-five. Several top-notch professions also had a mandatory retirement age requirement. They included air traffic controllers, airplane pilots, and the military. The consensus was that in these professions any decline in vision or hearing, any decline in the ability to endure stress, and the increased risk of medical emergencies would pose a grave danger to public safety.

There was no mention of any age limits in the Constitution. In that absence, some legal experts agreed that it would require passage of a Constitutional amendment to impose an age requirement on a federal judge or office holder.

"I don't know how you do that. You would have to amend the Constitution?" noted Republican Senator Richard Shelby of Alabama. In 2022, he was near age ninety, and he quickly fell back on the standard argument that a person just hitting a certain age didn't automatically mean their cognitive fitness would fall. "I think it depends on the person, too, a lot of times. I've known some people sharp in their mid-90s."

*****

The flip side of "how old is too old" is the impact that aging elected officials staying in office past their prime have on younger people who might desire to seek office. Some hold that their youth, instead of an asset, could be an impediment and thus a disincentive for them to enter politics.

In 2024, that was the concern of Georgia Democratic Senator Jon Ossoff, who at thirty-five was the youngest member of the U.S. Senate. "More important than those constitutional limits are the various structural impediments in our political system as it functions today that deter, and make it so difficult, and discourage young people from seeking office."

The number of younger people holding office and seeking office bears out this concern. In 2022, researchers on age and politics found a decided scarcity in the number of people thirty-five and under holding an elected office. They put the numerical gap of their gross under-representation in office at a factor of three in comparison to their percentage of the general population.

The paucity of younger people in politics was not just a problem in American politics. It was a problem in nearly every other country surveyed. "I think the old age of legislators is a problem," noted former New Zealand prime minister Helen Clark. "We have the world's largest generation ever of youth. So, if decisions are being made by an age cohort that is decades above that and is not attuned to their perspective, I think it's a serious democratic deficit. I used to be of the view that people needed to come into parliaments with some degree of maturity and background. I no longer think that. I think a parliament is a place where young people with fresh perspectives should be. And I think our political system should accommodate that."

The main reasons that the political systems she referred to didn't make accommodations for youth weren't hard to find. One was experience. Younger candidates who were fresh to politics lacked it. Part of that experience was the ability to raise money, secure endorsements, recruit seasoned staff to run a professional well-oiled campaign, and the ability to develop a core of key contacts and advisors. This high hurdle was raised even higher by the power of incumbency.

Often a younger person was matched up against a long- or longer-term serving incumbent. The incumbent had the money, clout, party imprimatur, and name identification. That made a huge difference in the ability to win and hold an office. This was even more of a disincentive for younger people to toss their hat in the ring for an office. It further fed the sense of alienation and disdain that many younger people had with politics and politicians.

Yet, when any cross-section of voting-age young people were asked about the reasons why they didn't vote or engage in any political activity, the allegedly out of touch because of their advanced age politicians were not one of the reasons cited. Almost always the reasons they gave were the same. The candidates didn't represent their views, no matter what their age. Other factors were that they frequently moved and were not informed about where their polling place was. Others cited heavy work or school schedules.

The litany of reforms that were proposed to ramp up the numbers of young voters likewise focused almost exclusively on addressing these logistical concerns and political differences. The age of the elected officials was not one of them.

9

The Gerontocracy of Political Power

There's yet another formidable barrier a young aspiring candidate for office must face. That's the seniority system within Congress. It is a powerfully stacked deck that older serving members use to consolidate their grip on both their office and the reins of governance. They obtain both just simply by staying in office.

The longer they stay, the higher they rise in the party and the congressional hierarchy. They're assured of plum House and Senate committee assignments and ultimately the control of those vital committees. This was a huge selling point an aging senator or House member used to assure continued backing from their constituents at election time.

That point wasn't lost on eighty-nine-year-old Iowa Republican Senator Chuck Grassley in 2022. By then he had served in the Senate for forty-one years. His campaign ads boasted that, if reelected, he would have the "most seniority in the entire Senate." He won overwhelmingly.

Backers of California Democratic Senator Dianne Feinstein continually made that fallback argument to ward off the loud calls for her to step down because of her mounting infirmities. One of her staffers put it best: a diminished senator representing California was "better than a junior" senator.

In 2022, New York Democrat Alexandria Ocasio-Cortez, age thirty-two, didn't buy this argument. "If you are on a committee and want to chair it, you basically have to wait until almost everyone before you resigns or leaves office. That often takes decades. So, people wait. And wait. And wait." She continued, "Those who DID wait and are in leadership (or next in line for it) are incentivized to protect the automatic seniority system as much as possible because of their sunk time cost."

Ossoff agreed: "Tenure yields power yields tenure," he said, referring to the campaign finance system, partisan gerrymandering, and the centralization of power within party apparatuses. "Some of the same dynamics that drive partisan polarization also make the political system less competitive. Those sorts of anti-competitive dynamics can make it more difficult for younger candidates to get a shot."

Ocasio-Cortez flatly called for an overhaul in the way Congress determines who should run a committee—a way that did not solely rely on who had sat in Congress the longest. Ironically, the GOP, not the Democrats, took some initiative in this regard. In the mid-1990s, the GOP slapped a clamp of six years on how long one of its members could hold the chairmanship of a House committee.

The Democrats punted repeatedly on the issue and declined to impose any limits. The GOP move was a good step forward and did result in some turnover in committee chairs. The subsequent turnover was just enough to allow younger congresspersons without the requisite long-term seniority and age to assume the mantle of committee chair power.

*****

There was also the issue of an age limitation in reverse. Age thirty or thirty-five is the legal minimum requirement for running for many top American elected offices. On the surface that seems like a reasonably fair age requirement. The downside is that it sent a subtle signal that age was a factor in running for an office. The under-thirty age group was excluded.

The proposals usually put forth to incentivize younger persons to run for office invariably came back to such things as term limits, dropping the age requirement to age eighteen, and for the Democratic and Republican parties to set age quotas for candidates and incumbents to run and hold office. None of these proposals ever got past the talking stage. Given the intense vested interest in older elected officials continuing to seek reelection, the likelihood was that those proposals would remain stillborn.

As mentioned, the Founding Fathers never seriously took a hard look at age as either an asset or an impediment to holding office. There was no mention of it in the Constitution. However, some of the Framers weren't unmindful of the issue. Their general sense was that age was equated with maturity and sound judgment, the two seemingly key requirements crucial in decision-making.

George Mason—one of Virginia's delegates to the Constitutional Convention of 1787, for instance, noted that, "political opinions at the age of twenty-one were too crude and erroneous to merit an influence on public measures." James Madison was even more explicit on the alleged relation of age to maturity and decision-making. He noted the "more advanced age" of Senators and then insisted in the unsigned *Federalist No. 62* that the "nature of senatorial trust" required a "greater extent of information and stability of character," and that age thirty represented a "period of life most likely to supply these advantages."

The debate about youth versus age centered squarely on whether age (either young or old) was a plus or a minus, or neither. The bottom line had always been that it was still an individual thing. Some older people retained their mental and physical sharpness. Some younger people had neither. Duke University professor James Chappel put it less delicately: "There are plenty of people who are younger than Joe Biden who are way dumber than him."

There was some slight irony in that the best-known aging elected officials, including Jimmy Carter and Mitch McConnell who had cognitive and physical challenges due to aging, did not dismiss term and age limitation requirements out of hand. Grassley, who did vote for term limits, didn't hesitate when asked if he would vote for it again: "Yes, I would vote for it again." McConnell, who voted twice for term limits, presumably also hadn't changed his view in 2022, saying "It's fair to ask about anything reasonable, including age." Carter, who backed an age limit requirement, simply said that he would not be up to the task of the presidency at eighty years old.

Before she died in 2023, Feinstein was the elected official who re-ignited the sharpest debate over an age requirement. She was slightly ambivalent about an age limitation, saying "I've had a lot of life and I've seen a lot of people die very young, and so I think age is just something that you contend with."

There was little doubt that Feinstein's quip would never cease being a flash point issue as long as America's elected officials kept getting older and older. Likewise, any and every sign of a mental or physical slip on their part would almost always become hot news. In 2024, Biden remained the prime example.

10

What Other Countries Say and Do About Their Aging Politicians

It was inevitable. The debate over Biden's age prompted a look at how other nations dealt with their aging politicians. There were marked differences, but also similarities. In 2023, European ministers and members of their parliaments were on average two to three decades younger than Biden and many members of Congress.

How much younger? Then German Chancellor Olaf Scholz had been in politics for more than three decades. At age sixty-four he was two decades younger than Biden. But even more revealing, he was only one of four European leaders over age sixty. The others were Nicos Anastasiades of Cyprus, Antonio Costa of Portugal, and Klaus Iohannis of Romania. He had been an elected politician since the 1990s. By contrast, nine of the twenty-seven other European leaders didn't come close to breaking age fifty. That continued a trend among European elected officials.

Since the 1980s, they had steadily gotten younger and younger. By contrast, in the 1950s the average age of Europe's elected officials was in the late sixties. By the mid-1980s the average age had plunged to the early fifties. There were several presidents and prime ministers who were in their thirties. They were less experienced in politics, did not rely exclusively on cash, endorsements, and support from the mainstream parties, and were super savvy about tech and social media.

There was much debate, though, about whether the youth trend in European politics was a plus or a minus. One political observer seemed to echo the sentiments of the majority, who felt that on balance European politics and governance did not suffer from having younger faces in European parliaments and higher office, saying "I would not say that European politics has suffered from an increasing number of younger and less experienced leaders. Instead, selecting younger leaders without typical long political careers has allowed parties to stay connected to voters and may have helped them to be more responsive to voter demands. Altogether, I wouldn't say that the rise of younger leaders has made the EU more dysfunctional."

*****

Many older American elected officials certainly disagreed with that. They continually argued that there was still much room for aged politicians, as long as they were fit. Biden was one example. But he was hardly the only aged elected official worldwide who was fit. In 2023, he was only the ninth oldest political leader globally. Meanwhile, in a Pew survey, Trump came in among the top twenty-five oldest among top elected officials among one hundred and eighty-seven member states of the United Nations.

The survey gleaned several key facts about the member nations' top political leaders, young and old in 2023:

- Their ages ranged from the mid-thirties to ninety. Several of the leaders in their thirties headed governments in Chile, Finland, and Montenegro. The oldest at ninety headed the Cameroon government.

- One-third of the top officials did have a few years on them. They were in their sixties. Five percent were in their eighties.

- On the downside many of the older leaders headed governments that were partially or fully authoritarian. Only two countries with leaders in their eighties were ranked "as free." One was the U.S. and the other was Namibia.

- More countries had increasingly more women heading the top political posts. They were younger on average than their male counterparts.

- It wasn't just Biden who was far older than the median age of in his country. That trend held in other countries as well. Andorra, Montenegro, Italy, and Finland were some of the countries where the top politico was younger than the median age of their country's residents.

- Norway had the greatest proportion of youthful elected officials worldwide. Nearly fifteen percent were under thirty. That compared with less than one percent of U.S. elected officials. There were twenty-three representatives in Norway's national assembly, the Storting.

In interviews on the aging issue and politics, a number of these young, elected officials eagerly gave their views on holding office and recounted their experiences. They agreed that it was important for elected officials to reflect as closely as possible the median age demographic of their country's residents. They further agreed that there were problems that ranged from climate change to gun violence that younger politicians in office could provide fresh approaches to and a willingness to tackle.

In the absence of the continued infusion of youth into politics, Amanda Litman, co-founder of Run for Something, a group that supports progressive candidates under forty, warned that this exclusion would further feed "a cycle of cynicism" and disengagement. That cycle in American politics, with few exceptions, was well in evidence in most elections in the U.S. since the 1960s.

The refusal of Biden, and to a lesser extent Trump, to bow to age and step aside in the presidential derby had another consequence. It sparked a mild backlash. Several polls found that voters were insistent that they wanted some fresh new faces to vote for in the presidential race other than Trump or Biden.

The underlying inference was age was a major reason for that wish. How much their disenchantment was with the lack of that fresh face would only be determined when the final 2024 presidential vote tally was in.

<h1 style="text-align:center">11</h1>

Workout Baby Workout

"It's hard to get into a regular schedule, but for me, I've been sticking to a routine, and it helps. It helps me deal with my day. I try to get out of bed by eight o'clock in the morning and I have a gym in my house upstairs. I have a treadmill and a Peloton bike and some weights."

Biden then said that after he finished his daily workout, he topped it off with a protein shake. A knowledgeable observer added that during the COVID pandemic in 2021, his day usually started with a meeting, somewhere between forty minutes and an hour and a half, with the medical staff who were dealing with COVID.

Biden disclosed his workout schedule in an interview on the campaign trail in 2020. If the interviewer, in this case Michigan Governor Gretchen Whitmer, hadn't asked him the question about his fitness routine he almost certainly would have eagerly volunteered his schedule. This was not just a pithy question about his fitness routine that departed from the weighty political issues.

Biden needed to assure the by-then-growing legion of Biden-age detractors that he had a routine to stay fit. There was little doubt that age and Biden's physical fitness would be a constant concern and even a point of attack by the GOP during the campaign. A regular exercise routine was his obvious pushback.

Yet, for Biden, it was more than using exercise as a prop to brush back the constant nitpicking about his age.

Medical experts and physical therapists agreed that aging did take a toll on the musculature system. Atrophy was an inevitable part of the toll taken. Weight resistance work was the proscribed means to strengthen the muscles and increase mobility.

Biden's physical exams released in 2021 and 2023 didn't indicate any symptoms of atrophy. The only thing close was a stiffness in his walk from a combination of arthritis in his back and neuropathy in his feet. Neither of these conditions indicated any physical impairment.

To maintain prime muscular fitness Biden didn't just lift weights, he used adjustable dumbbells to increase and decrease the effort and muscular resistance. Weakening muscles in older adults is a prime cause of slips and falls, and issues with balance, walking, and movement. All of these were the signs of aging that Biden critics closely watched for any hint of.

*****

The obsession with Biden's age and fitness had become such a hot topic in the run-up to the 2024 presidential election that one major daily newspaper even tracked down a handful of Biden's key staff personnel. They were familiar with his daily routine. The point was to determine how active he really was and how much stamina he had.

They confirmed that Biden did indeed have an almost daily routine of weightlifting, stretching, time on an exercise bike, and walking on a treadmill. His fitness routine was supervised by a private trainer. The staffers ticked off a wide range of activities, meetings, briefings, and events that filled Biden's day. It appeared to be taxing enough.

However, this wasn't enough to silence the chronic Biden age watchers. One was then-House Minority Leader GOP Congressman Kevin McCarthy. He dredged up the stamina issue or his alleged lack thereof to question Biden's fitness for the office. "At no time, having known Joe Biden for quite some time, does he have the energy of Donald Trump. Donald Trump didn't need to sleep five hours a night, and he would be engaged."

McCarthy and other Trump boosters took great delight in continually comparing Trump's alleged vigor to Biden's alleged feebleness. Both men had submitted to detailed medical exams. The results were publicly released before the presidential election in 2020. These disclosed that both men had small irregularities, but overall for men their age, they were declared fit.

The big difference that McCarthy omitted about Trump was that Biden had a regular fitness workout routine. Trump didn't. Biden's weight was a relatively trim one hundred eighty-four pounds for his nearly six feet height. Trump's near two-hundred-and-fifty-pound weight was hardly the healthy norm for his age and height.

*****

Unlike Biden, Trump's exercise routine often seemed to consist of how fast and how much energy he expended eating junk food. Trump and exercise were an oxymoron. At one point during his tenure in the Oval Office, his lack of exercise alarmed his White House physician. He noted, "He's more enthusiastic about the diet part than the exercise part, but we're going to do both." The good doctor confessed that Trump was inching toward obesity.

Trump quickly disputed the doctor, "I get exercise. I mean I walk, I this, I that. I run over to a building next door. I get more exercise than people think." CNN poked fun at Trump's so-called exercise regimen:

1. Walking

2. This

3. That

4. Run to building next door

5. Unspecified number of repetitions

Trump wasn't finished. He turned the exercise obsession on its head making the case that his lack of a tough, regular fitness routine was a plus. "A lot of people go to the gym, and they'll work out for two hours and all. I've seen people … then they get their new knees when they're fifty-five years old and they get their new hips, and they do all those things. I don't have those problems." He still wasn't finished. He put another fresh spin on what he considered exercise. He claimed that his long-winded orations before audiences were real work and therefore as he put it, 'That's exercise.'"

Trump's peculiar view of what constituted exercise wasn't anything new. He had often made pejorative cracks about exercising which he thought was a waste of time since it only wore the body down and, according to his expert opinion, one's body had only so much energy or as he put it "life force." He warned one of his business cronies who was training for an Ironman Triathlon, to knock it off, saying "You are going to die young because of this."

*****

Trump could have stretched things and made the case that his many hours spent on the golf course could be counted as exercise. He didn't bother with that rationale since he did little to no walking between holes. His method of exercise between the holes was riding in a golf cart. He had a ready rationale for that, too: "I don't want to spend the time to walk."

Trump, though, would not be one-upped on the issue of his non-exercise in contrast to Biden's enthusiastic and regular exercise program. He bragged that he shocked everyone with his fitness during his annual physical exam: "I was on a treadmill for the first time actually in quite a while, and it was at a very steep angle, and I was there for a very long time. They were surprised. And they said, 'Well you can stop now, that's amazing.' And I said, 'I can go much longer than this if you want me to.'"

Trump's braggadocio about his physical prowess seemed to conform to the assessment of one of his physicians during the 2016 presidential campaign. He claimed, "If elected, Mr. Trump, I can state unequivocally, will be the healthiest individual ever elected to the presidency."

This was of course blatant over-the-top hyperbole. It did point up one thing though. Biden and Trump had polar opposite views on the importance of fitness and exercise. Yet, neither one could be said to be mentally or physically challenged because of their age.

12

Too Old Doesn't Mean
Too Ignored

The picture of a voter casting his ballot during the 2018 midterm elections was standard and familiar viewing fare in newspapers and magazines. The voter almost always was an older man This was not by chance. In the 2018 midterm, voters aged sixty-five and older overwhelmingly made up the majority of those who voted.

In the 2022 midterms, nothing changed. Voters aged sixty-five and older still cast the almost identical percentage of majority votes as in 2018. Voters aged fifty-plus also determined the winner and loser in more than sixty of the closest races for the House.

The retort was that this was not unusual for off-year elections when younger voters were far less likely to vote. That trend supposedly reversed itself in the presidential election. There was some, but only some, truth to that. More younger voters aged eighteen to thirty generally did vote in a presidential election. However, proportionately, the age group that still delivered the largest number of votes was those sixty-five and older.

While the debate raged over whether Biden and Trump were too old for the Oval Office, the truth was that both men more closely reflected the age demographic of the majority of American voters than younger presidential candidates. That remained true for the 2024 presidential election.

*****

Biden and Trump, indeed all politicians, do two things best. They count dollars. And they count votes. Those voters who are most likely to show up at the polls are going to get the closest ear of elected officials.

Older voters have long had the closest thing to a monopoly on the attention of elected officials as a particular voting bloc can get. That translated to elected officials being attuned to the issues that seniors were most concerned about.

For decades the two issues at the top of that list have been Social Security and Medicare. Democrats Franklin Roosevelt in the 1930s and Lyndon Johnson in the 1960s were the architects of those two programs. Through the years, there have been countless efforts to tweak, cut, reshape, and in the more extreme cases eliminate the programs. Each time there was a storm of protest from seniors. Each time the proposals for change have been sharply modified or outright defeated.

The tip-toe by politicians around tampering with Social Security was on classic display during the administrations of three presidents. The first was George W. Bush in 2005. At the prodding of conservative GOP legislators and Wall Street, he proposed partially privatizing the system.

The stated goal was to give younger workers more financial say-so in handling their retirement money. This would have been a windfall for Wall Street investment houses. The near consensus from many public policy analysts was that if the plan had been enacted it would have been a disaster for the workers who withdrew their money from the system to engage in risky investments.

Predictably, the proposal touched off a huge backlash from senior citizen advocacy groups, most Democrats, and more than a few Republicans. They recognized the political peril for the GOP in the proposal. It was dropped.

Next up was Democrat Barack Obama in 2012. He did not go the privatizing route. Instead, he established the high-sounding, but cautiously neutral, bipartisan National Commission on Fiscal Responsibility and Reform. It didn't matter. It was tasked with examining the long-term financial sustainability of programs such as Social Security. The result was the same. It went nowhere. Again, senior citizen advocacy groups smelled a red herring in the proposal. They viewed it as a sneaky backdoor ploy to shrink Social Security.

By contrast, Republican Trump appeared to grasp the folly of drastic tampering with the program. He called it political suicide to mess with the program. On the other end, Democrats quickly recognized the extreme political danger of pushing too hard for shrinking Social Security.

Instead, they continued to search for ways to shell out more money to seniors. They saw this as a surefire-winning political formula. The proposals generally involved raising the wage cap on who would pay and increasing the payroll tax. The burden would fall heaviest on higher-income earners and businesses.

*****

Tampering with Medicare posed even more peril than Social Security. The program directly impacted the health and wellness concerns of seniors. It encompassed access to and the ability to pay for quality health care. This was a priceless commodity for seniors. Trump didn't mince any words in assuring there would not be any drastic modification of Medicare. He publicly vowed to defend it with "every ounce of his strength."

This was not simply more Trumpian over-the-top bluster. The ongoing debate over escalating medical healthcare costs and the recurring fears of the system going bankrupt continued to be major concerns. Both Republicans and Democrats tipped cautiously around any talk of reducing benefits, increasing taxes, or even shifting the costs and programs to private providers.

Instead, they searched for alternatives that posed no political danger.

They included such things as value-based care initiatives. That would permit Medicare plans to offer chronically ill enrollees nonmedical services, such as home-delivered meals and transportation, and move more services out of clinical settings and into the communities where people live.

But as with any program change, there are winners and losers. Medicare and Social Security were the long-term winners. The losers would be the tradeoff of big slashes in non-defense discretionary programs such as education, housing, jobs, and environmental protection programs. Spending on them would be drastically cut or pared back. These are the programs that are more shorter term, but directly benefit younger persons—that is, younger voters.

*****

Both Social Security and Medicare were so intimately tied to aging that the mere mention of reforms instantly raised red flags. Both were most seen by older voters as the programs that played the most pivotal roles in guaranteeing their interests. "It is easier for older people to see the relevance of government in their lives. Two of the biggest federal spending items, Social Security and Medicare, are conferred largely based on age," noted Massachusetts Institute of Technology political science professor Andrea Louise Campbell. "For the nonelderly, it can be harder to recognize the relevance of government because it's hidden behind hard-to-see regulation or hidden in the tax code." She could have also added that persons younger than sixty-five years old for the most part do not see the importance of these programs in their lives.

It was not just age and the number of older people who were more likely to vote than younger people. It was also their location and stable residence. Younger people were far more likely to move than older persons. They were far more likely to be renters, share housing, or live at home with their parents. When a younger person changed residences, they were required to register again within their new precinct. This was a major disincentive for many younger people to register, let alone vote.

"Younger people move much more than older people," said Harvard University government professor Stephen Ansolabehere. "Older people are much more likely than the younger people to be registered, and that explains most of the correlation of voting with age." The issue of residence and voting for younger people was only the start of a larger problem. Older people who lived in the same location for many years or decades knew when and where to go to vote.

"When people are in a community for a long time as homeowners or long-time residents," Tufts University political science professor and author of *Politics Is for Power*, Eitan Hersh, noted, "they start to feel more connected to the political process. They don't have to re-register to vote. They don't have to learn a new polling location or method of casting a ballot. Voting eventually becomes a routine." A retiree also had more time and leisure to go to a polling place or even to mail in their ballot.

Younger workers had to look carefully at the clock to determine if and when they could vote in person or by mail. Then there were the senior citizen advocate organizations. There was no such organization comparable to the AARP among younger persons. The AARP and other senior advocacy organizations filled up their publications with meaty information on the major issues that affected seniors.

Social Security and Medicare changes always ranked at the top of that list. This made a huge difference in terms of spurring older voters to engage with elected officials, and in turn for elected officials to engage with them. "Older Americans have mobilizing organizations like AARP who inform them about the role of government and their stake in public affairs," noted Campbell. "There are few equivalent mobilizing and information-providing organizations for the nonelderly."

*****

The second thing that politicians pay the closest attention to, in addition to who votes, is who pays. That means money. Elections are costly. The higher up the electoral food chain, such as the House and especially Senate races, money becomes a dominant factor in who wins and who loses. These races require millions to be raised and spent.

Even local and state offices can be fierce, competitive, and thus costly. The money must come from somewhere, apart from the major donors, the unions, and corporations. That somewhere is the campaign contributions from those individuals who can afford to contribute. Those most likely to have the financial means to kick in the cash are older voters. In the 2020 presidential election year, those aged seventy and over possessed a disproportionate share of the nation's wealth, more than thirty percent.

A Federal Reserve survey found that by 2020 the aggregate wealth of Americans aged seventy or more had jumped six-fold to more than forty-three billion dollars. That amounted to the staggering figure of five trillion in equity holdings alone. Overall, nearly forty percent of the nation's corporate equities and mutual fund shares were held by people aged seventy and older. This was the highest amount of wealth ever held by older people. In contrast, the wealth of those younger had risen only about two point five times higher. Older people were also more likely than younger persons to have substantial stock market holdings.

When the question was repeatedly asked and debated about how old is too old in politics, another question also had to be asked and answered: who votes and who pays? These are the two greatest questions that determine why politicians manage to stick around as long as they do, and why they are most keenly attuned to the issues that older voters (who bankroll much of American politics) demand that they pay the closest attention to.

The proof: in 2018 an AARP poll focused on older voters in swing districts named Social Security (83%), Medicare (79%), and health care (79%) as the most important factors influencing their votes. That was not likely to change.

13

Rethinking Ageing in Politics and Beyond

There was a curious sidenote to the furious debate and worry over whether Biden and Trump are too old to be battling for the presidency, let alone hold the presidency. That was whether age, as with race and gender issues, pitted one generation against another. In 2024, it was hard to skirt the issue since Americans were markedly getting older and were living longer, and in many cases living healthier.

As mentioned repeatedly, whether in commercials, ads, media depictions, films, popular articles on aging, and political campaigns, older people were thought of and treated differently than younger persons. The terms that were most often heard to describe this treatment regarding older persons were "marginalized" and "ignored." Many, maybe even a majority of Americans, regarded aging and the aged as sickly, dependent, and in more extreme views a drain on public and health services.

One observer zeroed in on this problem, "The over-fifty crowd that TV viewers are exposed to—particularly in commercials—are generally suffering from various forms of dysfunctional body parts requiring an abundance of medication whose side effects are listed in excruciating detail, further solidifying the image of weakness."

True, older aged, elected officials were careful not to alienate senior advocacy groups or do anything to downsize

Medicare and Social Security. Yet there was no concerted effort by policymakers to create or back programs and policies that directly addressed the problems and needs of older people.

The two critical areas of public policy that would always be problematic and cried for the need to be addressed were healthcare and employment discrimination. Though Medicare was enshrined as untouchable, that untouchability didn't apply to the costs. The estimate in 2020 was the one-year cost of the program was more than sixty billion dollars. That figure almost certainly would continue to climb in the years that would follow.

*****

Numerous studies and surveys found that many older people aged sixty-five and older were capable and desired to continue working. However, that did not mean that employers were any more ready or likely to hire them no matter how fit and qualified they were. A rash of state and federal laws prohibited workplace discrimination based on age.

But how could one prove that an older applicant didn't get hired because of their age? The legal bar was way too high to prove that in most cases. That remained an area that required public policy education, changes, and greater enforcement.

Medical experts, senior advocacy groups, and public policy experts on aging continuously tried to reverse the mostly negative thinking of large segments of Americans about aging. They continually implored the public and elected officials to regard aging not as a curse but as a vital resource of experience, productivity, and contribution. Unfortunately, in many cases that had the opposite effect. It reinforced the message and belief that the aged were somehow different, and that the difference was negative and something to be avoided.

"This is largely because these messages cue the public's ingrained negative patterns of thinking about aging," observed one medical expert, "that include a sense of fatalism that the problems are too big, the solutions are too complex, and that investment elsewhere would be more effective." To change that would require a total revamp of the ways the messages about aging were conveyed or, better still, reframed. The biggest challenge in the reframing was breaking through the implicit bias and stereotypes of the aged. That included the language and terms commonly used to describe older people, which would require a sharp reversal in thinking.

*****

The debate over Biden's age and the presidency was a near textbook example of that need for a reversal. The drumbeat characterization of Biden was always "too old," "too prone to gaffes and slips," and "too endangered from falls." A reversal in the media and public depiction of him would have been to characterize Biden as a fitness fanatic.

Biden made dozens of speeches and interviews almost all with flawless delivery and grasp of facts and policy details. He covered much ground daily walking without tripping, slipping, or falling. The job of the presidency is one of the most physically and mentally demanding jobs on the planet.

Biden's wife, Jill, confirmed that the toll the office takes wasn't just confined to the man in the Oval Office, saying "The job is twenty-four hours a day. I think it's a little harder than I imagined. It's not like a job that you do; it's a lifestyle that you live, and it's not something you leave at 5:00 or 3:00 … it's twenty-four hours a day."

"Aging experts and advocates will need to be vigilant of messages that describe older people as deserving special treatment," insisted Patricia M. D'Antonio, Vice President of Professional Affairs for the Gerontological Society of America. "Rather, we need to emphasize our common experiences as people who are aging and conversely, our uniqueness as individuals moving along the life course."

Rethinking the issue of aging in politics entails rethinking the issue of aging in daily life. That applies to everyone, no matter what their age, simply because aging is an inescapable part of everyone's life—not just Biden's life and the presidency.

14

How The Founding Fathers Saw Age and Politics

"**A**rticle II of the Constitution doesn't set a maximum age for holding the office of president, instead setting a minimum age of thirty-five and stringent citizenship requirements as the preconditions for executive power."

The fact that the Founders set no upper age limit on the presidency was curious. One of the principal Founders, the nation's first president and the man who wears the mantle "The Father of Our Country," George Washington thought he was too old to hold just about any office. He was then what would be considered today almost a spring chicken in the "too old to be president" age debate. He was aged fifty-one. He believed that he was washed up physically and resigned from his military commission in 1783. He famously said that he was "not only gray but almost blind in the service of my country."

This almost certainly was an exaggeration. However, Washington even at fifty-one had topped by a decade the average life expectancy of men in those days. Washington also may have been looking over his shoulder at two of his Fellow Founders, Alexander Hamilton and Edward Rutledge. Hamilton was age thirty and Rutledge was age twenty-six. Rutledge had a pronounced bias against the old men whom he felt had outlived their day, saying "Great Britain has passed the Meridian of her Day. We are young." This was not youthful braggadocio. Nearly all the Founders were younger than Washington, in their thirties and early forties.

*****

Washington was not alone in recognizing the seeming importance of youth in making weighty political decisions. Thomas Jefferson at seventy- one could not have been more explicit on this notion. "Our machines have now been running for seventy or eighty years, and we must expect that, worn as they are, here a pivot, there a wheel, now a pinion, next a spring, will be giving way."

University of Torino history professor Mauricio Valsania examined the thinking and writings of the Founding Fathers on aging. He observed that though being in one's seventies in the eighteenth century was positively decrepit, still the Founders didn't dismiss old age as a liability.

In August 1776, a debate about designing a new great seal for the republic took place. A commission was formed, and Benjamin Franklin, a member of the commission, proposed to draw Moses, with his wand lifted, in the act of dividing the Red Sea, and the pharaoh, in his chariot, overwhelmed with the waters. Franklin also suggested a motto: "Rebellion to Tyrants is Obedience to God."

Moses was Franklin's pick, said Valsania, because he represented veneration, sage knowledge, and vigor in his battle against tyranny. Franklin also may have felt kinship with Moses for another reason. Franklin at age eighty-one was one of the oldest of the Founders, a French witness held. He looked like a sage, a living classic "contemporary with Plato," as if he had come directly from "the age of Cato and Fabius."

Even though America's two best-known Founders, Washington and Jefferson, publicly disparaged old age, that did not mean they were ready to personally throw in the towel. Washington served two terms as president, beginning when he was almost sixty, and though nearing seventy offered to take up arms again in the military in the event of a feared war against the French.

The septuagenarian Jefferson stayed busy as he put it with "the Hobby of my old age." He put a massive amount of his time and energy into the building of the University of Virginia. That effort was a major factor in turning the school into a first-class center for higher education.

*****

There was yet another reason why the Founders, though they may in some cases have personally looked askance at old age in politics, did not put any age ceiling in the Constitution for the presidency. They had a jaundiced view of someone whom they regarded as too young taking over the top spot.

One of the Founders, George Mason, used himself as a prime exhibit of the potential danger of someone too young and immature in the Oval Office, "If interrogated," he said, he'd "be obliged to declare that his political opinions at the age of twenty-one were too crude and erroneous to merit an influence on public measures." Mason was sixty-two at the time.

He argued strenuously for a minimum, but no maximum age requirement. But Mason did not have the only word on this. Another of the Founders took a different view. James

Wilson thought it was wrong to exclude someone from the top spot solely because of their youth.

He insisted that this would "damp the efforts of genius, and of laudable ambition. There was no more reason for incapacitating youth than age, where the requisite qualifications were found." The Founders didn't agree with that sentiment. A drafting committee settled the matter when it voted seven to three to set the minimum age limit for the presidency. It was silent on any ceiling age limit.

James Madison, who was one of the great architects in the framing of the Constitution, also had serious qualms about the wisdom of having someone deemed too young to hold a major office. In this case, Madison singled out senators. In the *Federalist No. 62*, he declared that a qualification for the Senate should be advanced age. As he put it, "senatorial trust" demanded a "greater extent of information and stability of character ... that the senator should have reached a period of life most likely to supply these advantages."

Another principal Founder, James Monroe, had a different concern. He believed that if someone deemed too young was eligible for the top spot, that would pave the way for building a family dynasty. "The Constitution has provided, that no person shall be eligible to the office, who is not thirty- five years old; and in the course of nature very few fathers leave a son who has arrived to that age."

As mentioned previously, the irony of the perfunctory age debate among the Founders was that a dozen of them at the Constitutional Convention were under the age of thirty-five. That meant that not one of them by their age eligibility mandate would have been eligible to run for president.

Then there was the man who penned the draft Declaration of Independence in 1776, Thomas Jefferson. He was all of thirty-three at the time.

The Founders in the end sent a mixed message in the "too old for the presidency" debate. They were young. Many admired and praised the vigor of youth—but not to the point of imposing no minimum age requirement for the presidency.

On the other hand, they had reservations about the potential liability of old age and holding a political office. But not to the point of putting an age ceiling on who could hold a political office. That was first and foremost the presidency.

Conclusion

How old were the Democrats running in the 2024 election?

- Joe Biden: 80

- Marianne Williamson: 71

- Robert F. Kennedy, Jr: 69

How old were the Republicans running in the 2024 election?

- Donald Trump: 77

In April 2023, *USA Today* was so concerned about whether the leading candidates were too old to be elected President that it asked a panel of experts on politics and aging to weigh in on the issue. It first cited a *USA Today*/Suffolk University poll that found that nearly forty percent of both Democratic and Independent voters said that Biden's age made them less likely to vote for him.

Biden though could take comfort in the poll's other finding. Nearly sixty percent of voters said his age made no difference to them. It also noted that a significant number of voters said that they'd like to have a "fresh" face to vote for. They did not equate that fresh face with age. However, the inference of age was there.

The experts offered up the by-then well-worn, familiar arguments and questions about age and the presidency that had been entombed in the age debate since Biden first declared he was a presidential candidate in 2020. They boiled down to the issues of stamina and mental alertness.

However, other experts countered with the same arguments that Biden and a slew of medical experts cited. That is Americans were living longer, living healthier, and that if they could do a job with no drop-off in their mental sharpness and ability then there should be no reason why someone, in this case Biden, should not seek another term.

There was also a pragmatic reason for a Biden second term run. A survey of presidential elections found that when a sitting President does not opt to run for a second term his party comes up short in holding the White House. To be more exact, it lost the White House in eight of twelve elections.

"His GOP opponents knock the President's age, while their frontrunner is almost the same age, and shows far more signs of mental decline," noted John A. Tures, LaGrange College professor of political science. "Democrats should stick with Biden, and not panic at early adverse surveys."

*****

But there was a caveat. Another medical expert cautioned that voters should pay close attention to an aged candidate or officeholder for any sign of a physical and cognitive lapse in their fitness. This caveat was softened by assuring that while many septuagenarians and octogenarians do experience significant physical and cognitive declines, many others do not.

The experts reiterated what had become the well-known mantra of the 2024 presidential campaign. That was that

Biden would be eighty-two at the start of his second term if reelected. Trump would be seventy-eight at the start of his term if reelected.

Trump though, with an obvious glance over his shoulder at those who might raise the issue of whether he, like Biden, was too old to hold the presidency, came to Biden's rescue: "There are many people in their eighties, and even nineties, that are as good and sharp as ever. Biden is not one of them, but it has little to do with his age. In actuality, life begins at eighty!"

Trump's ringing endorsement of the possible glories of old age would never stymie the relentless debate about how old is too old to hold an office, particularly the presidency.

Even if Biden's age was not an issue for most voters, and they were totally satisfied with his physical and cognitive fitness, that would not likely prevent many from continually wondering quietly and out loud during his White House tenure about his fitness.

Any gaffe, blunder, flub, stumble, or in the worst-case scenario, a fall, would ignite an explosion of media and public chatter, reportage, and endless speculation, even proof for many, that Biden or Trump was just "too old."

The *National Enquirer* was a near textbook example of that in October 2023. Even though there was no immediate report of a Biden slip, stumble, or gaffe, that didn't stop the *Enquirer* from compiling a checklist of quotes from varied observers on Biden's alleged mental and physical failings.

Retired U.S. Army General Paul Vallely said, "Biden's physical and mental capacity seem to diminish with each passing month." He then added that he felt it was "embarrassing to have a leader who appears so infirm on the world stage."

Next in the door was Dr. Gabe Mirkin, a longevity expert, who said "If you look at his face, you will see significantly increased wrinkling and loss of facial fat, both of which are indicators of advanced aging." Then there was Dr. Carole Lieberman, who works as a forensic psychiatrist in Beverly Hills and has experience in determining mental competency, who noted that Biden's "memory loss or lapses, rambling speech, poor impulse control, and irritability" were becoming worse.

It ended with the almost obligatory citing of alleged worries about Biden's fitness, always from unnamed Democrats. "Some senior Democrats privately were frustrated with Biden's advance team for months, citing the [Air Force Academy] sandbag incident and noting that the president often appears not to know which direction to go after he speaks at a podium."

Despite feigning that he had no issue with Biden's age, Trump just couldn't resist getting yet another lick in at Biden's age. This time he retweeted on his *Truth Social* social media platform a fake ad that characterized the White House as "a senior living facility." The narrator declares, "Our vibrant facility offers delightful activities and outings, round-the-clock professional care, and exquisite house-made meals." It piled it on further by showing clips of Biden on a beach in Delaware with his wife helping him put on his coat and opining that he needed "professional care."

*****

Biden and Trump, though, performed a public service just by their dogged determination to retain or regain the Oval Office. They forced many Americans to confront the issue of age in politics. They forced many more Americans to admit that age did not automatically consign the aged to a life of inevitable mental and physical deterioration.

Biden and Trump could take heart from the legion of medical experts who insisted that they did not see any sign or proof that either one of them had lost their work capacity and their ability to perform what is arguably the most demanding political job in the world at a high level of competence. Unfortunately, that would not be enough to diminish the age and ageism obsession in American politics and beyond.

Postscript

"'Going to get worse': Ex-WH doctor warns pace of Biden's cognitive decline already putting US 'at great risk.'"

The instant Biden turned eighty-one in November 2023, a former White House physician under Bush, Obama, and Trump, now turned GOP congressman, Ronny Jackson, rushed in to again claim that Biden's age should be an issue of concern.

"[The decline is] happening quickly," Jackson told a Fox News interviewer. And just how did he know that? "As you said, I've taken care of three presidents... so I know firsthand what it takes to be the commander-in-chief and the head of state. It's a grueling job, both mentally and physically. This man can't do the job. He's proven to us every single day that he can't do the job, but this is going to get worse."

This wasn't the first time that Jackson rang the warning bell about Biden's alleged mental failings. The big difference was that he didn't stop there. He demanded that Biden submit to a cognitive test. If he refused, Jackson called for him to fold up his tent for the 2024 presidency.

"It's just unbelievable how much he's degenerated just during his time in office. We cannot afford to have this man in office for the remainder of this term and then [for] another four years after that. He's already putting us at great risk right now," he self-righteously declared.

Jackson allegedly bolstered his case against Biden by ticking off the crucial issues that confronted the country and that demanded a president be in full possession of his faculties to handle.

"[Look at] the wars that we're getting drawn into. Things that wouldn't happen if Donald Trump were there because our enemies don't fear us anymore. They have no respect for us anymore and our adversaries don't trust us anymore, and it's because we don't have the leadership in the White House that we need," he said.

"It's because this man, even if he wanted to, he cannot provide that leadership. He is not physically and cognitively fit for office anymore, and somebody in his inner circle needs to step up to the plate and make him aware of this, and he needs to move on for the safety and security of this country."

Jackson in a relatively short period in the interview managed to get all the negative talking points against Biden in the mix—mental failing, incompetent, danger to the country, unable to function, and drop out.

Rest assured, Biden would be hit with these and more damning indictments every moment of campaign 2024.

Sources

Introduction

Anna Halkidis, "Ronald Reagan's Epic Response When Asked About His Age During a Debate," *Little Things*, October 21, 2015, https://littlethings.com/lifestyle/ronald-reagan-epic-debate-moment.

History.com, "Reagan and Mondale in 1984 Presidential Debate," https://www.history.com/speeches/reagan-and-mondale-in-1984-presidential-debate.

Rachel Schilke, "Biden rejected by Democrats as 40% of his party doesn't want him to run again," *Washington Examiner*, n.d., https://www.msn.com/en-us/news/politics/biden-rejected-by-democrats-as-40-of-his-party-doesnt-want-him-to-run-again/ar-AA1kiTO3.

https://www.msn.com/en-us/news/politics/biden-celebrates-his-81st-birthday- with-jokes-as-the-white-house-stresses-his-experience-and-stamina/ar- AA1kfUNf.

1 How Old is Too Old

Ben Gittleson and Molly Nagle, "Joe Biden announces he is running for president again, setting up possible Trump rematch," *ABC*, April 25, 2023, https://abcnews.go.com/Politics/joe-biden-running-reelection-2024- setting-trump-rematch/story?id=98801535.

The World Health Organization, "Ageing and Health,"
The World Health Organization, October 1, 2022,
https://www.who.int/news-room/fact-sheets/
detail/ageing-and-health.

The Net Worth Of, "Biden Showing Early Signs of
Alzheimer's? 'Repeats Himself word-for-word…is
He Even Fit for Office?'" *The Net Worth Of*, n.d.,
https://www.msn.com/en-us/news/politics/biden-
showing-early-signs-of- alzheimer-s-repeats-
himself-word-for-wordis-he-even-fit-for-office/
ar- AA1hRSy6.

Noah Berlaisky, "Let's fact check Biden's so-called mental
decline," *Independent*, July 11, 2023, https://
www.independent.co.uk/voices/biden-fact-check-
mental-decline-b2373172.html.

Marc Sigel, "Should the nation be concerned about Biden's
cognitive abilities?," *The Hill*, January 31, 2022,
https://thehill.com/opinion/white-house/591990-
should-the-nation-be- concerned-about-bidens-
cognitive-abilities/.

2 The War on the Aged

Clickinsights, "5 Commercials That Reinforced Ageism
with the Worst Stereotypes," *Clickinsights*, June
20, 2022, https://www.clickinsights.asia/post/5-
commercials-that-reinforced-ageism-with-the-
worst-stereotypes.

Ken Dychtwald and Robert Morison, "How Ads Do a
Terrible Job Portraying Older Adults," *nextavenue*,

July 14, 2020, https://www.nextavenue.org/ads-portraying-older-adults/.

Tom Spiggle, "Proving Age Discrimination Is Hard—But Possible. Here'sWhat Workers Need to Know," *Forbes*, May 16, 2022, https://www.forbes.com/sites/tomspiggle/2022/05/16/recoverable-damages-in-an-age-discrimination-employment-case/?sh=37d4f31c48b9.

Romeo Vitelli, "Exploding the Myths about Aging," *Psychology Today*, July 1, 2020, https://www.psychologytoday.com/us/blog/media-spotlight/202006/exploding-the-myths-about-aging.

Betsy Klein, "Biden's birthday prompts debate about age and wisdom of America's oldest president," *CNN*, November 20, 2023, https://www.cnn.com/2023/11/20/politics/joe-biden-birthday-81/index.html.

Bryan Robinson, "Ageism: Taming the Last Frontier Of Career Discrimination," *Forbes*, December 5, 2023, https://www.forbes.com/sites/bryanrobinson/2023/12/05/taming-the-last-frontier-of-career-discrimination/?sh=3f7f8607583e.

Rebecca Knight, "I'm a 56-year-old laid-off IT worker looking for a job. I have a hunch I'm not having luck due to ageism. How do I prove it?" *Business Insider*, March 27, 2023, https://www.businessinsider.com/how-can-older-workers-prove-ageism-and-age-bias-in-hiring-2022-11.

David Weissner, "US House members propose lower bar to prove workplace age bias claims," *Reuters*, December 4, 2023, https://www.reuters.com/legal/government/us-house-members-propose-lower-bar-prove-workplace-age-bias-claims-2023-12-04.

3 The Democrats' Jitters Over Biden's Age

Reuters, "US Vice President Harris dismisses Biden age concerns, but ready to be president, *Reuters*, September 7, 2023, https://www.reuters.com/world/us/us-vice-president-harris-dismisses-biden-age-concerns-ready-be-president-2023-09-07/.

Kevin Liptak, et.al., "Biden tells donors he's 'not sure I'd be running' in 2024 if Trump wasn't in the race, *CNN*, December 5, 2023, https://www.cnn.com/2023/12/05/politics/biden-fundraising-sprint/index.html.

Rozina Sabur, "Joe Biden's Democratic challenger angers party with critique of Kamala Harris," *The Telegraph*, December 22, 2023, https://news.yahoo.com/joe-biden-democratic-challenger-angers-192439831.html?fr=sycsrp_catchall.

Jill Filipovic, "Critics say Biden is old and tired. But so is his most likely opponent, Trump," *The Guardian*, August 30, 2023, https://www.theguardian.com/commentisfree/2023/aug/30/biden-trump-age-presidential-election-2024.

Heather Hamilton, "Democratic strategist walks back comments questioning Biden's 2024 chances,"

Washington Examiner, November 7, 2023, https://
www.washingtonexaminer.com/news/campaigns/
david-axelrod- walks-back-comments-biden-
2024-chances.

Ken Dychtold, "Ageism is alive and well in Advertising,"
AARP, November 8, 2021, https://www.aarp.org/
work/age-discrimination/ageism-in- advertising/.

4 Fun and Games with Biden's Gaffes, Stumbles, and Fumbles

Tess Alps, "Why advertisers will always target the
young," *The Guardian*, October 10, 2005, https://
www.theguardian.com/media/2005/oct/10/
mondaymediasection9.

Darlene Supperville, "Biden says he got 'sandbagged'
after he tripped and fell at Air Force graduation,"
AP News, June 1, 2023, https://apnews.com/
article/biden-fall-trip-air-force-stage-sandbag-
794279498487420486000171770e33bc9.

Sara Dorn, "Biden Slips on Air Force One Stairs After
Staff Try to Prevent Major Falls—As Gaffes Raise
Concerns About His Age," *Forbes*, September
26, 2023, https://www.forbes.com/sites/
saradorn/2023/09/26/biden-slips-on-air- force-
one-stairs-as-his-team-tries-to-prevent-major-
falls-as-trips-and-gaffes-raise-concerns-about-his-
age/?sh=729f202b3e94.

Tom Boggioni, "'Stunned' former Trump official alarmed
by his 'lack of sharpness' at Iowa rally," *Alternet*,

December 3, 2023, https://www.alternet.org/
stunned-former-trump-official-alarmed/.

Rachel Frazin, "Biden indicates he would only serve one
term as president: report," *The Hill*, December
11, 2019, https://thehill.com/homenews/
campaign/474027-biden-indicates-he-will-only-
serve-one-term-as-president-report/.

Jonathan Martin, "Senior Democrats' Private Take
on Biden: He's Too Old," *Politico*, February
16, 2023, https://www.politico.com/news/
magazine/2023/02/16/senior-democrats-joe-
biden-old-00083129.

5 Reagan Got the "Too Old" Knock, Too

"Ronald Reagan's Age as President: A Comparative
Analysis," *The Politics Watcher*, September 24,
2023, https://thepoliticswatcher.com/pages/
articles/white-house/2023/9/25/ronald-reagan-
age-president-comparative-analysis.

Andrew Glass, "Reagan Undergoes Cancer Surgery, July
13, 1985," *Politico*, July 13, 2010, https://www.
politico.com/story/2010/07/reagan-undergoes-
cancer-surgery-july-13-1985-039636.

Christopher Lane, "When Did Reagan's First Signs of
Alzheimer's Appear?" *Psychology Today*, January
21, 2022, https://www.psychologytoday.com/us/
blog/side-effects/201101/when-did- reagans-first-
signs-alzheimers-appear.

VOA, "Reagan Challenged Notions He Was Too Old to be President - 2004- 06-11," *VOA*, October 29, 2009, https://www.voanews.com/a/a-13-a-2004-06-11-28-1- 67349872/272923.html.

Lou Cannon, "Age Emerges as New Issue in Campaign," *Washington Post*, October 20, 1984, https://www.washingtonpost.com/archive/politics/1984/10/10/age-emerges-as-new-issue-in-campaign/87ce695b-e233-4cc9-82c5-8ff1b3c894a0/.

Andrew Glass, "Reagan recovers in second debate," Oct. 21, 1984," *Politico*, October 21, 2018, https://www.politico.com/story/2018/10/21/this-day-in-politics-oct-21-1984-910774.

6 McCain Got the "Too Old" Knock, Too

AP, "Murtha says McCain Too Old to be President," *NBC News*, April 16, 2008, https://www.nbcnews.com/id/wbna24162740.

CBC News, "McCain medical records show skin cancer concern, healthy heart, *CBC News*, May 23, 2008, https://www.cbc.ca/news/world/mccain-medical-records-show-skin-cancer-concern-healthy-heart-1.695507.

Newsweek Staff, "Alter: Obama vs. McCain," *Newsweek*, February 16, 2008, https://www.newsweek.com/alter-obama-vs-mccain-94135.

Garry South, "The Age of McCain," *Politico*, August 20, 2008, https://www.politico.com/story/2008/08/the-age-of-mccain-012884.

Frank Newport, "General Election Shaping Up as Change vs. Experience" *Gallup*, June 4, 2008, https://news.gallup.com/poll/107671/General-Election-Shaping-Change-vs-Experience.aspx.

Liz Halloran, "McCain's Age and Past Health Problems Could Be an Issue in the Presidential Race," *US News*, May 9, 2008, https://www.usnews.com/news/campaign-2008/articles/2008/05/09/mccains-age-and-past-health-problems-could-be-an-issue-in-the-presidential-race.

Zachary B. Wolf, "They're 80+. They're in charge. They're not going away," *CNN*, September 25, 2021, https://www.cnn.com/2021/09/25/politics/older-dc-politicians-what-matters/index.html.

Joshua Sharp, "Obama's Attack on McCain's Age Immature," *CBS News*, September 19, 2008, https://www.cbsnews.com/news/column-obamas-attack-on-mccains-age-immature/.

Brian Montopoli, "Critics Try to Make McCain's Age and Issue," *CBS News*, May 22, 2008, https://www.cbsnews.com/news/critics-try-to-make-mccains-age-an-issue/.

Early and Often "The Real Reason McCain's Age Might Matter," *Intelligencer*, August 15, 2008, https://nymag.com/intelligencer/2008/08/the_real_reason_mccains_age_mi.html

Alan Silverlieb, "Analysis: Age an issue in the 2008 Campaign?" *CNN*, June 15, 2008, https://www.

cnn.com/2008/POLITICS/06/15/mccain.age/
index.html.

7 It's Not Just Biden—US Politicians are Old

Zachary B. Wolf, "They're 80+. They're in charge. They're
not going away," *CNN*, September 25, 2021, https://
www.cnn.com/2021/09/25/politics/older-dc-
politicians-what-matters/index.html.

Mychael Schnell, "House Democrats call for Feinstein to
resign, *The Hill*, April 12, 2023, https://thehill.
com/homenews/house/3947037-house-democrat-
calls-for-feinstein-to-resign/.

Anthony Zurcher and Sam Cabral, "Mitch McConnell
freezes for second time during press event," *BBC*,
August 31, 2003, https://www.bbc.com/news/
world-us-canada-66665682.

Mary Kate Cary, "Why are US politicians so old? And why
do they want to stay in office?" *The Conversation*,
December 23, 2023, https://theconversation.com/
why-are-us-politicians-so-old-and-why-do-they-
want-to-stay-in-office-217024.

Brad Ryan, "Why are America's politicians so old—and
does age matter in politics?" *ABC*, September 3,
2023, https://www.abc.net.au/news/2023-09-03/
us-ageing-politicians-mconnell-feinstein-biden-
trump/102802482.

Nancy Jecker, "There's no age limit for politicians—
as people live longer, should that change?,
The Conversation, August 28, 2023, https://

theconversation.com/theres-no-age-limit-for-politicians-as-people-live-longer-should-that-change-211318.

8 Should There Be an Age Limit for Politicians?

Jennifer DePinto, "CBS News Poll: Big Majority Favor Maximum Age Limit for Elected Officials," *CBS News*, September 8, 2022, https://www.cbsnews.com/news/elected-officials-maximum-age-limits-opinion-poll-2022-09-08.

Steve Chapman, "Bernie Sanders is Too Old," *Chicago Tribune*, Feburary 5, 2016, https://www.chicagotribune.com/politics/ct-bernie-sanders-is-too-old- 20160205-story.html.

Tanner Stenning, "Should there be a maximum age limit for elected politicians?" *Northeastern Global News*, July 31, 2023, https://news.northeastern.edu/2023/07/31/elected-politician-age-limit/.

John Jackson, "71 Percent of U.S. Senators Out if Age Limits Imposed on Elected Officials," *Newsweek*, January 20, 2022, https://www.newsweek.com/71-percent-us-senators-out-if-age-limits-imposed-elected-officials-1671314.

Anna Chodos, "The case against age limits for politicians," *Stat*, October 4, 2023, https://www.statnews.com/2023/10/04/age-limits-white-house-congress-mcconnell-biden-trump-feinstein/.

Karen Turner, "The often-overlooked reasons why young people don't vote," *Vox*, October 15, 2020, https://

www.vox.com/21497637/election-2020-youth-vote-young-people-voting.

9 The Gerontocracy of Political Power

Aksel Sundstrom, "Politicians are getting older–shutting young people out of decision-making around the world," *The Conversation*, January 5, 2023, https://theconversation.com/politicians-are-getting-older-shutting-young-people-out-of-decision-making-around-the-world-197140.

Bryan Metzger, "There's overwhelming support for an age limit on the president and Congress. Here's why that won't happen anytime soon," *Business Insider*, December 24, 2022, https://www.businessinsider.com/congress-term-limits-age-gerontocracy-old-lawmakers.

David Smith, "Too old to govern? The age problem neither US party wants to talk about," *The Guardian*, September 3, 2023, https://www.theguardian.com/us-news/2023/sep/03/old-age-mcconnell-biden-trump-politics.

10 What Other Countries Say and Do About Their Aging Politicians

David Hutt, "Europe's leaders are younger and less experienced. It probably doesn't matter," *Euronews,*January 9, 2023, https://www.euronews.com/my-europe/2023/01/09/europes-leaders-are-younger-and-less-experienced-it-probably-doesnt-matter.

Laura Silver, "As Biden considers reelection bid, who are the oldest–and youngest – current world leaders?" *Pew Research Center*, March 24, 2023, https://www.pewresearch.org/short-reads/2023/03/24/who-are-the-oldest-and-youngest-current-world-leaders/.

Sam Cabral, "What Congress can learn from country with youngest lawmakers," *BBC*, October 6, 2022, https://www.bbc.com/news/world-europe-63068931.

Lauren Walker, "As many under 30s in European Parliament as people called 'Martin,'" *The Brussels Times*, September 14, 2022, https://www.brusselstimes.com/289640/as-many-under-30s-in-european-parliament-as-people-called-martin.

11 Workout Baby Workout

Ashley Parker, "Weightlifting, Gatorade, birthday calls: Inside Biden's day, *Washington Post*, May 24, 2021, https://www.washingtonpost.com/politics/biden-daily-routine-gatorade/2021/05/23/b6f608c2-b40e-11eb-a3b5-f994536fe84a_story.html.

Melanie Kaidan," Go hard! Joe Biden's impressive daily fitness routine includes weightlifting and shakes," *Express*, May 4, 2021, https://www.express.co.uk/news/world/1431389/joe-biden-fitness- routine-us-president-morning-workout-potus-health-ont.

James Bickerton," How Joe Biden's Physical Compares to Donald Trump's," *Newsweek*, February 16, 2023, https://www.newsweek.com/how-joe-bidens-physical-compares-donald-trumps-1781809.

Matt Evans, "Joe Biden uses dumbbells and cardio workouts to lose weight at 78," *Fit and Well*, December 1, 2021, https://www.fitandwell.com/news/-joe-biden-workouts-0305.

Graham Lanktree," Donald Trump Just Revealed His Surprising Exercise Regime," *Newsweek*, January 18, 2018, https://www.newsweek.com/trumps-exercise-regime-amazing-784250.

Michal Kranz, "How past presidents' exercise routines compare to Trump's," *Business Insider*, January 18, 2019, https://www.businessinsider.com/trump-exercise-president-workout-routines-obama-bush-clinton-2018-2#when-trump-plays-golf-he-drives-a-golf-cart-during-the-campaign-trump-also-said-he-viewed-rallies-as-a-form-of-exercise-2.

12 Too Old Doesn't Mean Too Ignored

Emily Brandon, "Why Older Citizens are More Likely to Vote," *US News*, October 5, 2020, https://money.usnews.com/money/retirement/aging/articles/why-older-citizens-are-more-likely-to-vote.

AARP, "How Older Adults are Changing America," *AARP*, September 1, 2023, https://www.aarp.org/politics-society/history/info-2023/older-adults-changing-america.html.

Alex Tanzi, "Americans Over 70 Hold More Than 30% of the Country's Wealth," *Bloomberg*, n.d., https://

www.msn.com/en-us/money/personalfinance/
    baby-boomers-over-70-hold-more-than-30-of-
    wealth-in-the-us/ar-AA1lKJrI.

13 Rethinking Aging in Politics and Beyond

Lauren Stiller Riklee, "Why Young People Need to
    Look at Older People Differently," *Forbes*,
    January 21, 2016, https://www.forbes.com/
    sites/nextavenue/2016/01/21/why-young-
    people-need-to-look-at-older-people-
    differently/?sh=5b1126f45742.

Nora Super, "Three Trends Shaping Ageing in
    America," *Oxford Academic*, April 20,
    2020, https://academic.oup.com/ppar/
    article/30/2/39/5822709?login=false.

Oma Seddeq, "First Lady Jill Biden dismisses questions
    about the president's mental fitness as 'ridiculous,'"
    Business Insider, December 9, 2021, https://www.
    businessinsider.com/jill-biden-concerns-about-joe-
    bidens-mental-fitness-are-ridiculous-2021-12.

Patricia D'Antonio, "Reframing Ageing in Contemporary
    Politics," *OUP Blog*, October 22, 2020, https://
    blog.oup.com/2020/10/reframing-aging-in-
    contemporary-politics/.

Jeff Mason, "Biden, 80, is healthy, 'fit for duty,' doctor
    says after physical, *Reuters*, February 16m 2023,
    https://www.reuters.com/world/us/biden-80-
    have-closely-watched-physical-exam-2023-02-16/.

14 How the Founding Fathers Saw Age and Politics

Maurizio Valsania, "80 is different in 2023 than in 1776–but even back then, a grizzled Franklin led alongside a young Hamilton," *The Conversation*, April 25, 2023, https://theconversation.com/80-is-different-in-2023-than-in-1776-but-even-back-then-a-grizzled-franklin-led-alongside-a-young-hamilton-202812.

Jared Keller, "Is Bernie Sanders Too Old to be President?" *Pacific Standard*, March 1, 2019, https://psmag.com/social-justice/should-there-be-an-age-cap-on-the-president.

Scott Bombay," Why does a presidential candidate need to be 35 years old anyway?" *National Constitution Center*, July 22, 2016, https://constitutioncenter.org/blog/why-does-a-presidential-candidate-need-to-be-35-years-old-anyway.

Conclusion

John Tures, "Why the odds are in Joe Biden's favor for a second term as President | Opinion," *Palm Beach Post*, November 9, 2023, https://www.palmbeachpost.com/story/opinion/columns/2023/11/09/why-joe-biden-should-run-for-a-second-term-and-not-step-aside/71491907007/.

Sudishka Kochi, "Are some candidates too old to be running for president? How age will play a role in the 2024 campaign," *USA Today*, n.d., https://

www.msn.com/en-us/news/politics/are-some-
candidates-too-old-to-be-running-for-president-
how-age-will-play-a-role-in-the-2024-campaign/
ar-AA1f4Roo.

Lauren Irwin, "Trump shares 'White House senior living'
ad trolling Biden," *The Hill*, January 13, 2024,
https://www.aol.com/trump-shares-white-house-
senior-201419460.html.

Postscript

https://www.msn.com/en-us/news/politics/going-to-
get-worse-ex-wh-doctor-warns-pace-of-biden-
s-cognitive-decline-already-putting-us-at-
great-risk/ar-.

Bibliography

Attia, Peter. *Outlive: The Science and Art of Longevity.* Kindle Edition 2023.

Bernstein, Jonathan (ed.), *The Making of the Presidential Candidates 2024.* New York 2023.

Binstock, Robert H. and James H. Schulz. *Aging Nation: The Economics and Politics of Growing Older in America.* 1st Ed. New York, 2008.

Burns, Alexander and Jonathan Marin. *This Will Not Pass: Trump, Biden, and the Battle for America's Future.* New York, 2022.

Campbell, Colton C. and Mitch McConnell. *Leadership in the U.S. Senate: Herding Cats in the Modern Era.* 1st Ed. New York, 2018.

Cannon, Lou, President Reagan: *The Role of a Lifetime.* New York, 2000.

Chang, Joseph. *The Aging Myth: Unlocking the Mysteries of Looking and Feeling Young.* New York, 2011.

Coleman, Vernon. *Dementia Myth: Most Patients with Dementia are Curable.* New York, 2019.

Drucker, David. *In Trump's Shadow: The Battle for 2024 and the Future of the GOP.* New York, 2021.

Foer, Franklin. *The Last Politician: Inside Joe Biden's White House and the Struggle for America's Future.* New York, 2023.

Heilemann, John and Mark Halperin. *Game Change: Obama and the Clintons, McCain and Palin, and the Race of a Lifetime.* New York 2010.

Kashi, Robert, et.al. *Aging in America: The Years Ahead.* New York, 2003.

Hutchinson, Earl Ofari. *President Trump—Again?* Los Angeles, 2023.

Kra, Siegfried. *Aging Myths: Reversible Causes of Mind and Memory Loss.* 1st Ed. New York, 1986.

Lee, Brandy X. and Robert Jay Lifton. *The Dangerous Case of Donald Trump: 27 Psychiatrists and Mental Health Experts Assess a President.* New York, 2017.

Levitin, Daniel J. *Successful Aging: A Neuroscientist Explores the Power and Potential of Our Lives.* New York, 2020.

Murphy, Scott. *The Term Limit Revolution.* Kindle Edition 2017.

Orr, Tamara B. *Obama vs. McCain and the Historic Election.* Perspectives Library: Modern Perspectives. Kindle Edition 2017.

Seery, John. *Too Young to Run? A Proposal for an Age Amendment to the U.S. Constitution.* College Park, PA, 2011.

Utter, Glenn. *Youth and Political Participation: A Reference Handbook.* Contemporary World Issues. New York, 2011.

Whitehouse, Peter J. *The Myth of Alzheimer's: What You Aren't Being Told About Today's Most Dreaded Diagnosis.* New York, 2008.

Will, George F. *Restoration: Congress, Term Limits and the Recovery of Deliberative Democracy.* New York, 1993.

About the Author

Earl Ofari Hutchinson is the author of multiple books on race and politics in America. He is a political analyst. He has appeared on MSNBC and on CNN. His books include the trilogy on the Obama Years: *The Obama Legacy, How Obama Governed: The Year of Crisis and Challenge,* and *How Obama Won.* His most recent books are *The Trump Challenge to Black America, From King to Obama: Witness to a Turbulent History* and *Bring Back the Poll Tax—The GOP War on Voting Rights.*

Index